Cliff's Notes

on the

Science of Mind Textbook

by Rev. Cliff Rubin

WalkAcrossFire Publishing
5424 Newcastle Ave
Suite 369
Encino, CA 91316

(828)318-3389

First edition: September 2014

Paperback ISBN: 978-0-692-27986-1

Printed in the United States of America.

Contents

Introduction 1

Introduction: Part I-The Thing Itself 5

Chapter 1: The Beginning 13

Chapter 2: Mind...The Greatest Discovery 15

Chapter 3: Spirit 19

Chapter 4: Soul 23

Chapter 5: Body 27

Chapter 6: [Our] Relationship to the Spiritual Universe 29

Chapter 7: Summary of Part One: The Nature of Being 35

Chapter 8: The Power of Thought 39

Chapter 9: Prayer 45

Chapter 10: Faith 47

Chapter 11: Mental and Spiritual Treatment 51

Chapter 12: Summary of Part Two: Spiritual Mind Healing 59

Chapter 13: Causes and Conditions 61

Chapter 14: Physical Perfection 65

Chapter 15: Physical Perfection, Concluded 75

Chapter 16: The Principles of Successful Living 95

Chapter 17: Mental Equivalents 101

Chapter 18: The Law of Attraction 109

Chapter 19: Summary of Part Three: The Practice of Spiritual Mind Healing 117

Chapter 20: What the Mystics Have Taught 125

Chapter 21: Some Phases of the Subjective Life 133

Chapter 22: Finding the Christ 139

Chapter 23: Immortality 143

Chapter 24: General Summary 147

Introduction

This is a book of my commentaries on one of the greatest accomplishments of the twentieth century, the Science of Mind Textbook by Dr. Ernest Holmes. Dr. Holmes had a radio show for over twenty years which began with the phrase,"There is a power for good in the universe and we can use it." He wrote the Science of Mind Textbook to explain what this power is and how we can use it. This book is my interpretation of his teachings. It is also, what might be considered the "Cliff Notes", as I follow the textbook chapter by chapter, quoting, what I consider, the important points.

I am not declaring any special expertise on this subject, except as someone who has studied Dr. Holmes teachings for almost twenty years and has recently graduated the Holmes Institute as a Licensed Religious Science Minister. This is the church Dr. Holmes founded over seventy five years ago.

Over the years, as I have described these teachings, many of the questions asked were to clarify something in the textbook. The feedback I received over and over was to put my clarifying comments in a book. I heard that suggestion enough times to finally realize this was mine to do.

The best part about writing this book was reading each section until I felt I understood it well enough to explain what I had read in a way that would make sense to anyone. Many times this meant reading a section several times. Each reading led to a deeper layer of understanding of what this great man was sharing with us. What Dr. Holmes had to say is incredibly brilliant. I have done my best to translate his brilliance in a way that works for you.

Much love, time and effort went into this project, which became more of a journey as I walked the path of Science of Mind through the mind of Dr. Ernest Holmes. In many ways, it was like walking an incredibly large and complex labyrinth leading to the center of my own soul. I felt my own way of seeing the world challenged, more than once, with a new sense of self emerging. I have seen amazing changes in my life as it is impossible to immerse yourself in such a depth of power without that power being used to create a magnificent life. I believe, through this book, I have opened the door to that great labyrinth and given you a key, a way in, that might support your journey to a greater self and a life that uses this "power for good in the universe."

This book is not meant as a replacement for the Science of Mind Textbook, but as a companion guide, not only offering clarity, but a personal angle on Dr. Holmes' teachings. The commentaries are written in several ways. First, by the quotes I chose. They are not always his most famous, but the ones that spoke to me. Second, the use of partial quotes to emphasize a particular point I wanted to make. And, lastly, by adding my own thoughts wherever I felt that they enhanced or clarified a point. Also, I have, wherever possible, changed Dr. Holmes' verbiage to be more gender inclusive.

Another important point to make about my approach to this book and your understanding of what I have written, has to do with what some call the Four Kingdoms of Consciousness.

These are different levels of consciousness, awareness or understanding about who we are. The first is "to me". This is where we feel victimized by life, thus, life is being done "to me". The second is "by me". This is where we feel empowered to take action on our behalf, control certain circumstances and take charge of our lives. This is where we put forth our will in our creative process. The next is "through me". This is where we see ourselves as a vessel of the Divine, opening ourselves to a larger power that some label as God. The Native Americans call this being the hollow bone. The final level is "as me". This is where we recognize that, because there is only One, we are not just a part of that One, but the wholeness of that One. As Rumi would put it, "You are not just a drop in the ocean, but the entire ocean in a drop."

I mention these levels because I believe it is time to recognize ourselves through an "as me" consciousness and that the Science of Mind is a magnificent path to embodying this Truth. Throughout the book, Dr. Holmes expresses the subtle differences between taking responsibility for our lives from a "by me", "through me" and "as me" perspective. I have done my best to emphasize those points while focusing primarily on the "as me" perspective, using the others for contrast.

If you are a beginner to these teachings and have felt victimized by life, then "by me" is a brilliant start. Empowering yourself in any way you can, willfully or not, is an important first step. The recognition that we are not just these human bodies, but part of something much larger is a great second step and can lead to letting go of some of the burdens we think we must carry alone. A "through me" perspective allows for the unseen to enter our world and help guide our choices. This level of consciousness can open us up to what I believe to be the prime directive built into the very fabric of our being, which is Love, Harmony, and Wholeness. From this perspective we experience that all is One and we are some part of this One as is everything else, seen and unseen.

"As me" takes the perception of "through me" one step further. It is the level of conscious understanding that not only is there a Power that is larger than ourselves, yet still within us, but that this Power creates whatever we embody. It is the Truth that our lives are an immediate reflection of the totality of our thoughts, beliefs and actions, conscious and unconscious, at any given moment, and that by shifting that totality, we literally create a new experience, instantly. This totality I call embodiment and I use that word a lot throughout the book. In fact, because I believe that changing what we think is only the first step towards creating what we desire in our lives, I have, on many occasions, altered the verbiage in Dr. Holmes' quotes to reflect the embodiment that he and I agree are necessary for the desired result one seeks to show up in physical form. Any alterations I have made to Dr. Holmes' quotes are signified by

3

brackets. Embodiment and the "as me" consciousness are explained in much greater detail throughout the book.

There is a language, a jargon, that is used throughout Dr. Holmes' work. Learning this jargon will make it easier to understand what he is saying. A glossary is provided in the back of the Science of Mind textbook.

A book like this cannot be written alone. It takes quite a handful of incredibly enlightened individuals to create a commentary that might actually be useful to the masses. I, and a team of editors I am so, so grateful for, have done our best to that end.

First, I would like to thank Annette and Chuck Hunner, without whom this book would have never been realized. I want to thank my beloved Ashley Fuller for being the force that kept me moving as well as an incredible editor. Along editing lines, Carole Cross, Casey Conerly and Kathy Milam were invaluable for the effort and time they put into getting this project completed and making sure it was well written. I also want to thank all the folks at CSL of Greater Cincinnati for their encouragement to make this book a reality.

Last, but not least, I want to thank Dr.'s John and Barbara Waterhouse for introducing me to these teachings, treating my son and I like family and constantly challenging me to rise to my best.

It has been a privilege to have written this book. May you find in these teachings as much richness, depth and beauty as I.

Introduction: Part I-The Thing Itself

The thing to know about the Thing Itself is that there is only One. Everything in the universe and beyond it; infinite and everlasting; anything that ever was and ever will be; is the Thing Itself. We can call it God, Spirit, First Cause or any other name that strikes our fancy. It doesn't matter what we call it. What does matter is that we understand that this power encompasses everything, is Infinite, is beyond the beyond; and yet, It is right here with us, in us and as us in every moment. What matters is that we come to know that there is only One. This is what Dr. Holmes means, when he tells us, "The study of the Science of Mind is a study of First Cause, Spirit, Mind, or that invisible Essence, that ultimate Stuff and Intelligence from which everything comes, the Power back of creation— the Thing Itself (Holmes, 1938, p 26)."

This Power doesn't play favorites. It is equally everyone and everything. We are all this God Stuff, and because of this, have the Power to create. So, why do some create an abundant life filled with health, success, love, joy - and others a life of suffering? It is our understanding in how to use this Power that makes the difference. What we need to know about this Power is this: what we embody is what we create.

This Thing Itself, that we are and yet is much more than we understand ourselves to be, creates in the same manner that the universe, the stars and the earth were created. Our lives and every experience in our lives, is created out of the same God stuff as everything else that has ever been created or ever will be.

This Power is creating all of the time, whether we understand the Thing Itself or not. We don't have to be conscious of what Dr. Holmes calls the Subjective Mind or Mental Law for this Oneness to work. But, by developing our conscious awareness of this Power, we can direct what manifests in our lives through the use of this Power and thus create extraordinary lives. By directing "our individual use of that Greater SUBJECTIVE MIND, which is the seat of all mental law and action (Holmes, 1938, p 29)", we direct the course of our lives to the brilliance our lives have the potential to be.

This Subjective Mind is a creative mind, creating each moment of our lives whether we believe we are creating our lives or not. The deeper we can embrace that what we embody manifests, the deeper we delve into eradicating anything within our consciousness in discord to our alignment with what we want to create. This can be amazingly freeing. Free will at its best. We choose how much we wish to change.

So, what do I mean by what we embody? Our embodiment is the totality of our conscious and unconscious thoughts, beliefs, words, feelings and actions. The breadth and depth of all we embody is rather large unto itself. Which is what makes our growth an evolutionary process. "The evolution of man's consciousness brings with it the acquisition of new powers and higher possibilities (Holmes, 1938, p 32)."
The possibilities are endless. We do not just have the Power to create, *we are that Power that creates*, which is the Thing Itself.

Part II-The Way It Works

"[M]an's intelligence is this Universal Mind, functioning at the level of man's concept of It. This is the essence of the whole teaching. (Holmes,1938, p 36)" What Dr. Holmes is saying is that the only limitation we have in using this limitless power is the limitations we create in our own mind. If you believe your power to create is limited, it surely is!

Changing our perspective on how powerful we truly are may not be an easy task, but certainly one worth beginning. Catch yourself when you start thinking about the limitations of your life and instead focus on the infinite nature of who you truly are. Each day, spend more and more time thinking about your intention of what you want to create. Delve deeply into knowing that "There is a Universal Mind, Spirit, Intelligence, that is the origin of everything: It is First Cause. It is God (Holmes,1938, p 35)," and because this is true, that means we are this same Spirit, Intelligence, First Cause, individualized, yet one with this eternal Wholeness. As your beliefs in your limitations begin to shift, your perspective starts to expand. The more we become aware of this Power, which flows through us and is us, the more our lives manifest towards the extraordinary.

Shifting our beliefs is the key to the way the Law works. The sum total of all our thought, will, purpose, and belief, creates a tendency… "that causes [the Thing Itself] to react to us according to the sum total of that belief. (Holmes,1938, p 38)" The more time we spend believing that our lives work no matter our circumstances, the more the sum total of our beliefs shift. The more our beliefs shift to knowing our lives work, the more the circumstances shift to demonstrating our lives working. It really is that simple.

Part III-What It Does

"The Infinite Knowingness becomes our wisdom only in such a degree as we embody its Intelligence. (Holmes,1938, p 41)" "How much of this Reality are we going to express in our own lives? (Holmes,1938, p 42)" The answer, of course, is up to us. Each of us is using this Intelligence to create our lives all the time whether we are conscious of it or not. How conscious we are of doing so is completely in our hands.

There is, however, something built into the fabric of Infinite Intelligence. What Dr. Holmes calls, "Divine Givingness (Holmes,1938, p 43)," is evolving humanity to a greater and greater expression of Love. We are less barbaric, per capita, than at any other time in history. There are more people, per capita, on the planet who care about what happens to the rest

7

of humanity, who care about other species' well-being and survival, and who care about the environment and health of the planet, than ever before. How has humanity evolved in the direction of Love, if not by a directive, quiet enough to not interfere with our free will, but, persistent enough, to, when we willingly listen, know that within the core of our being, Love is who we long to be? This guiding directive is built into every cell of our being; expressing as us to the extent we are conscious of It and allow It. "Love is the Divine Givingness; Law is the Way (Holmes,1938, p 43)". Through "Divine Givingness" we express the true nature of Infinite Intelligence. We express God as Us. This is why we long for unconditional love. When we express it, and/or feel it, we feel at home.

As unique individuals, each of us opens to Infinite Intelligence from a different perspective. The painter perceives how to paint beauty and even within painting, the perception of beauty varies within painters. No one would confuse a painting by Van Gogh for one by Picasso. In every type of possible perspective, each of us hears, sees and experiences this One Source through the filter of ourselves. The further we can expand beyond our current perception, the more we awaken to the One we truly are. The more we awaken to the powerful Infinite Intelligence that we are made out of, the more we create from a sense of expansion. "But only as much of this Life as we embody will really become ours to use (Holmes,1938, p 44)".

Only we can limit the Power of Infinite Intelligence. No one else can do it to us. It might appear that we are limited by others, but that cannot be the Truth. There is no limit to the possibilities of how this Oneness might manifest in our world. There is no limit to the myriad of personalities and ways of being this One Mind can demonstrate Itself. There is no limit to how far we can expand our embodiment of our use of this Power.

What the Thing Itself does is create. As us, the Thing Itself is constantly, every moment of every day, creating. Built into the fabric of creation is the guiding light of Love. We are an expression of the Thing Itself, this Subjective Mind, this Infinite Intelligence and, as such, create our lives. The more active we are in aligning our beliefs, words, feelings and intentions with what we want to create, the more our lives become that which we intend them to be. "A passive meditation will never produce an active demonstration, any more than an artist can paint a picture by sitting down with his paints but never using them (Holmes,1938, p 47)".

Affirmative Prayer is the vehicle we use in Science of Mind to engage our creative process. We call our form of affirmative prayer "treatment." Treatment is defined as, "a statement in the Law, embodying the concrete idea of our desires and accompanied by an unqualified faith that the Law works for us, as we work with It (Holmes,1938, p 47)". This is more than hope. "Hope is good; it is better than despair, but it is a subtle illusion and is an unconscious compromise, and has no part in an effective mental treatment (Holmes,1938, p 49)". In treatment we hold in our minds an exact picture of what it is we want to create and know, not hope, that this picture is already created. This Subjective Mind, Infinite Intelligence, First Cause, God, is all giving, all knowing and, through the fabric of Love, acts on our behalf. "How much of this Infinite Good is ours? ALL OF IT! And how much of It may we have to use? AS MUCH OF IT AS WE CAN EMBODY (Holmes,1938, p 50)".

Part IV-How To Use It

The first thing to realize is that the Thing Itself is creating on our behalf all the time; every second of every day. Every thought we have is feeding the totality of the whole of our embodiment, which shapes the world we create. Every thought we have is creating something. The whole idea of treatment is to train our thoughts, which then feeds our beliefs, which then feeds what we embody, to work for what we want in our lives. This Infinite Intelligence is working, even when we think it's not working. "..if we believe that It will not work, It really works by appearing to "not work." When we believe that It cannot and will

9

not, then, according to the principle, It DOES NOT. But when It does not, It still does —only It does according to our belief that It will not (Holmes,1938, p 52)". So, even believing it does not work, has it working. Whatever you embody, this wonderful, creative force, which is us, will prove us right. "It is forever taking form and forever deserting the form which it has taken. Thus a practitioner of this Science should not be confused over any given form, but should know that any form which is not of the original harmony is subject to change (Holmes,1938, p 52)".

It doesn't matter what the circumstances currently are in the creative process. We can change them. In fact, everything in the physical universe is finite and is constantly changing. The practitioner knows the creative process is forever operating on our behalf and that all circumstances are in flux. The practitioner's job is to know the Truth and the Truth is that we are powerful, creative, spiritual beings creating our lives out of the One Mind, the Thing Itself, as us, and that what we can create is as Infinite as the Thing Itself. Anything less than this is not the Truth.

It is not that our circumstances are not real. It is that what takes physical form is re-created anew every moment and the moment we embody something different, something different becomes real. This is the difference between something we want showing up the moment we treat for it, like an instantaneous healing, or treating for something for years before it shows up. It all begins with our thinking, but, in the end, it is the totality of our embodiment that this unseen Powerful, Infinite Intelligence creates on our behalf. "In this invisible law of unfoldment, we must come to trust, and although we do not see the way, we must believe that the way IS and IS OPERATIVE. We must trust the Invisible, for It is the sole cause of that which is visible (Holmes,1938, p 57)".

The deeper we can embody this trust of the invisible and see ourselves as Source of our life experience, the more our lives unfold miraculously. In the science of Mind we propose that we "daily take the time to meditate and mentally treat the condition, no matter what the apparent contradictions may be (Holmes,1938, p 57)".

"A treatment is a spiritual entity… and is equipped with power and volition— as much power and volition as there is faith in it(Holmes,1938, p 58)". The deeper our embodiment, the more powerful the treatment. That is why we practice. It may take time to develop the capacity to align our entire being with the good we want in our lives. The good news is that practicing, in and of itself, begins change.

A weightlifter, who's dream is to press four hundred pounds, but, at the moment can only press one hundred pounds, will see improvement shortly after beginning to practice. It is the same with treatment. The more we practice aligning our thoughts towards creating what we want, the more we feed our beliefs. The more we feed our beliefs what we want, the more we shift what we embody. The more we shift what we embody, however slightly, what shows up in physical form reflects that shift.

No matter what the circumstance, "THE PRACTITIONER MUST KNOW, AND MUST STATE, THAT THERE ARE NO OBSTACLES IN THE PATHWAY OF TRUTH (Holmes,1938, p 59)". The Science of Mind textbook is a guide book towards this knowing and embodiment. "[T]his Science is the study of First Cause, Spirit, or the Truth, that Invisible Essence, that Ultimate Stuff and Intelligence from which everything comes— the Power back of creation— The Thing Itself (Holmes,1938, p 60)".

Chapter 1: The Beginning

Because "We wish to discover what to believe in, why we believe in it, and why such a belief is reasonable; and in so far as possible to enter into the nature of the invisible Cause of this manifest life of ours (Holmes, 1938, p 63)," we ask the question, "How did we and all other physical manifestations come into being (Holmes, 1938, p 63)?" The answer is, "SPIRIT MAKES THINGS OUT OF ITSELF THROUGH SOME INNER ACT UPON ITSELF (Holmes, 1938, p 63)." In other words, consciousness must be present for any creation to occur. Spirit, the Infinite Intelligence, always was and always will be and anything we can touch, hear or see must have come out and be made out of this same substance we call God, because that's all there is.

When we take a metaphysical look at the Bible creation stories, or, for that matter, any creation story, they all have something in common. That is they speak of an Infinite Power that began the process of creation and that process was started by an intention. In the Bible, it says, "In the beginning there was the word." Here, we can see the "word" as the guiding force that is behind all creation. Because God is infinite, so is God's word, which continues in the fabric of everything created.

This is as true for the One Mind as it is for our individualized minds. There can be no difference, because both are the same mind. "God cannot speak a word which contradicts [Its] own nature (Holmes, 1938, p 64)." Neither can we. "The world of multiplicity does not contradict the world of Unity, for the many live in the One (Holmes, 1938, p 69)." Each of us, everything of creation that has existed, does exist and will exist, lives in, and is made out of, the One. We are all unified with each other, because this Infinite Intelligence put forth the initial intention of creation, "THROUGH SOME INNER ACT UPON ITSELF (Holmes, 1938, p 63)," which infinitely recreates itself inside us and as us; today, tomorrow and always.

Chapter 2: Mind…The Greatest Discovery

We are the result of evolution. Over eons, different varieties of hominids, two legged creatures, have appeared on this planet leading to the two legged creatures we are today. We have a complex ability to think and understand our universe, its properties and the way it works, that continues to evolve over time. "Electricity was a reality in the universe when Moses led the children of Israel out of the land of Egypt, but neither Moses nor any of his followers knew anything about it. This is true of all natural laws; they have always existed but only when understood may they be used (Holmes, 1938, p 71)."

"The principle of any science is invisible, theoretical, as is our idea of Spirit. No one has seen God; no one has seen Life; what we have seen is the manifestation of Life. No one has seen Intelligence; we experience It. No one has ever seen Causation; we see what It does, we deal with Its effects (Holmes, 1938, p 72)."

It is through this Infinite Intelligence, this First Cause, God, that we are evolving. "The basis from which man is evolving is Infinite (Holmes, 1938, p 72)." There is no end to how far we might evolve. Each of us gets to choose, not only how much we evolve, but in what ways we evolve. We are all unique in our evolutionary process. That is why comparing ourselves to others is rarely helpful. What makes understanding this evolution important, is that it reminds us that whatever we think we understand about God and the creative process, it is constantly growing and shifting.

Memory is a double-edged sword. "… memory of itself is an unconscious operation of what was once a conscious thought (Holmes, 1938, p 74)." True creativity is always happening in the current moment. Once that moment has passed, and that moment is stored in memory, that memory may hinder or help our creative process, depending on what embodiment it reinforces. Remember, our lives reflect the totality of what we embody, which includes our conscious and unconscious memories.

"The Science of Mind, then, is the study of Life and the nature of the laws of [embodiment]; the conception that we live in a spiritual Universe; that God is in, through, around (Holmes, 1938, p 75)" and as us. The deeper we understand the "nature of the laws of thought" and our knowing God as us, the more we can embody what we want to create and the less we will create from our old memories and beliefs that may not serve us.

One of the ways we feed what we embody is by how we perceive our world. Reality is not set in stone. Because we perceive through the same Infinite Intelligence that created our perception, we are constantly at choice and can change our perception at any time. We are not talking about denying the very real experience one might be having at any given moment. But, there is always more going on than meets the eye and if we are willing to look beyond what appearances we can see at the present time, the limitless possibilities of the Infinite Intelligence open up to us. How we do this is addressed in much greater detail later on in the textbook. For now, please open to the possibility that what we believe to be real, may be much more pliable than we realize.

Because there is only One Mind, all thoughts by everyone are part of the same whole. This is what makes reading minds possible. "It is almost certain that between friends there is at all times a silent communication, a sort of unconscious mental conversation, going on. When this arises to the surface of the conscious intelligence, it is called mental telepathy (Holmes, 1938, p 77)." One day we might evolve where this becomes our primary tool of communication. But, presently, we still use the spoken or written word. Mental telepathy exists for us to discover and understand and may well be available in the future, like electricity was in the days of Moses, but is now a reality.

One of the more difficult aspects of the creative process to understand is that it is both a personal and impersonal process. It is personal from the standpoint that we choose what we want to create. It is impersonal from the standpoint that The Law, acting through Infinite Intelligence, simply says yes. It does not judge whether what we want is healthy or unhealthy, nor whether we are worthy of our desire. "There is a "Law in the Universe which operates in a certain way according to the tendency set in motion, and does so mathematically, inexorably (Holmes, 1938, p 78)." As we have stated, Infinite Intelligence takes the totality of all our conscious and unconscious thoughts, beliefs, memories and actions, and reflects them back to us in the life we experience. This process is re-created every moment of every day for everybody.

What we do understand about this process is the more we weigh in on the side of goodness, the more goodness shows up in our lives. This is a reality worth perceiving. We must keep nourishing our consciousness, in as many different ways as we can, for once the goodness weighs in, as the totality of what we embody, our lives will certainly reflect, in physical form, the miraculous life of our dreams.

We believe that God expresses as a Trinity of Being. This Trinity reveals itself as "God is Spirit, or Self-Knowingness; God is Law and action; God is result or Body (Holmes, 1938, p 80)." Thus, there is a three part process to creating: Our self-knowing, which is our embodiment; The Law or that part of God which takes our embodiment and creates; and Body or the physical manifestation that comes out of our embodiment. Through this Trinity and our understanding of it, our lives unfold. Understanding this Trinity will help with understanding some of the language or jargon used in the textbook.

Chapter 3: Spirit

In our Trinity description of God or Infinite Intelligence, Spirit is the self-consciousness part. It is the part that is aware of Itself and has the directives of Love and Goodness built into it. How do we know that Love and Goodness are built into the fabric of the One Mind? Because something deep in our being has moved civilization, over time, to be more civilized, more loving and less barbaric. A survey of history covering the last 5,000 years proves this out. There is less barbarism in the world today, per capita, than at any other point in history.

Because we have free will, this directive is a quiet voice that we get to choose to listen to or not. As we evolve, we become more and more aware of this gentle nudge towards a loving society. Even with free will, the reason we continue to evolve towards Love, is that this gentle nudge is as persistent and powerful as the waters that carved out the Grand Canyon. It may take time, but Love wins. "In moments of real inspiration, we realize, to a degree at least, that God is All— That which has within Itself all that really is— the Life in everything and the Love through everything (Holmes, 1938, p 82)."

So evil is not outside or somehow separate from the Infinite One. Through our free will, anything is possible to be created out of the many that are encompassed by the One, even what we might consider evil. This directive of Love is of a gentle nature, so as not to interfere with our free will, and yet, clearly exists.

"The Nature of First Cause is, that It is harmonious. If there were an element of [disharmony], discord or decay anywhere in Its Nature, It would destroy Itself (Holmes, 1938, p 83)." Everything created out of Spirit carries it's Nature of harmony. There is no creation out of nothing. Everything is created out of Spirit. Everything carries this directive of Love. It is up to each of us to open to this gentle nudging and allow

19

the directives of Love, Harmony and Goodness that mystics have been aware of through the ages, to permeate our day to day lives.

"All action must be some action of Spirit as Law (Holmes, 1938, p 84)!" This part of the Trinity, Law, is impersonal. It simply says yes. Our thoughts are the thoughts of Spirit, because everything is Spirit. The creative power we have is Law, which is still Spirit. The physical manifestation of what we have set forth to create is still Spirit. The only limitation in this Trinity is our conscious awareness of Its existence and how we use it.

"God, the Divine or Universal Life Principle, or whatever we choose to call It, is an Original, Uncreated, Changeless Being. Not a Being with parts, but BEING with potentialities (Holmes, 1938, p 85)." This is important to remember as we talk about the Trinity. We may use the word "parts" for understanding's sake, but a more accurate definition is potentialities. One of the basic tenets of quantum physics is that everything is an infinite potentiality or possibility until it collapses into an event or physical manifestation. It takes an Observer or Consciousness for a possibility to become a physical reality.

"The laws of Mind, or Spirit, are not different from the laws of chemistry and physics (Holmes, 1938, p 86)." They still must be tested and proved. It is through physical demonstration that we see the laws of Mind and Spirit at work. "Since we are dealing with that which is Limitless, knowing no big and no little, the possibility of our demonstration rests not in the Principle, but in our acknowledgment of, and embodiment in it, of the ideas we desire experienced (Holmes, 1938, p 86)!" As we expand what we embody, we expand our limitless ability to create. "No limit can be placed upon the spirit of man. It merges with the Universal Spirit for the two are really One (Holmes, 1938, p 87)." We are this Divine Nature. Each of us is the Trinity in our own right. Each of us is the totality of all that is Infinite only limited by our unique beingness; our unique self manifested out of and as the Divine.

This brings us back to the Love and Goodness that is built into Infinite Intelligence and thus, built into each of us and everything in creation. "PERSONALITY CANNOT EMERGE FROM A PRINCIPLE WHICH DOES NOT CONTAIN THE INHERENT POSSIBILITY OF PERSONALITY (Holmes, 1938, p 89)." This doesn't make Infinite Intelligence a being. It simply holds the possibility of beings to exist. It is through this sense of personality possibility that we personalize God. And, that is as it should be. "Spiritual evolution should make the Infinite not more distant; but more intimate (Holmes, 1938, p 89)."

Chapter 4: Soul

"Like the creative soil, in which seeds are planted and from which plant life comes, the Soul of the Universe is the Creative Medium into which the Word of Spirit falls and from which Creation arises (Holmes, 1938, p 90)." Out of the Soul of the Universe comes the Spirit that is our higher self; our larger self. It is beyond the physical and yet is still the individualized being that is each of us. "The term Subjective Mind [which is used throughout the Science of Mind textbook] is used in speaking of the Universal Soul, rather than the term Subconscious Mind, to avoid the impression that subjective means unconscious (Holmes, 1938, p 90)." This is because nothing in the All that is the Infinite Intelligence can ever be unconscious. Though, there is nothing unconscious in Subjective Mind, we, as individualized expressions of the Subjective Mind may be unconscious to the larger Spirit and, thus, the Universal Soul. But, It is not unconscious to Itself.

When we commune with our higher self, we are also communing with the One Mind. As we commune, our Soul recognizes what we have fully embodied and, in that moment, through the Law, speaks Its Word on our behalf, and returns to us, an exact reflection of our embodiment into physical form.

Our Soul is like a liaison with God. The Soul makes no choice for us on its own. It awaits our command. This is what gives us free will and allows us to make, what sometimes turns out to be, choices that are not for our highest and best good. But, within our Soul is the gentle nudge we've spoken of earlier, moving us towards Love and Harmony, if we choose to listen. This is what's called Divine Guidance.

"[T]he combined intelligence of the race could not create the life of a plant, yet the Intelligence in the creative soil of the earth will produce as many for us as we ask, when we plant the seed of that which we wish to have created (Holmes, 1938, p 92)." We cannot intellectualize creativity. It is built into the fabric of our being, executing each moment whether we think consciously of it or not. It is the soil awaiting our seed of embodiment, which we are planting anew each moment.

"If, through the Law, thought is creative, we cannot say that one thought will create while another will not. We must admit that all thought is creative, according to the impulse, emotion or conviction behind the thought (Holmes, 1938, p 94)." This is why it is so important to bring conscious awareness to what we think, feel, and believe. The reason it can feel like our lives are out of our hands, is because of all that is unconscious within us, affecting the creation of our lives. When we hear ourselves speak negatively about ourselves or others, even in jest, those words feed the creative process. This is an important point worth repeating. Everything we think, say, do or feel, conscious or unconscious, is constantly feeding the creation of our lives. The spiritual practice of denying the negative and proclaiming the Truth is immensely effective whenever we hear ourselves say or think something negative, not just as a ritual in the morning or evening. When we think, speak or feel anything that is in discord with who we want to be in the world, those are the moments where spiritual mind treatment can be the most powerful. Our lives are the reflection of the totality of what we embody. As we transform ourselves through spiritual practice, embodying what it is we wish to create, the more our lives reflect back to us, in physical form, the transformation of our embodiment. The more we catch ourselves thinking, feeling or acting against our own desires and re-state what it is we really want, the deeper we transform what we embody and thus, bring into form the life of our dreams.

Race consciousness can affect what we create as well, if we go along with it unconsciously. "Anything that has ever been thought at any time in the history of man, exists today in a subjective state in Universal Mind. When we get into the field of Mind, there is no past, present or future. They merge into one medium (Holmes, 1938, p 95)." People like Jesus, Gandhi and Martin Luther King understood they were making a stand to

24

evolve the race consciousness of their time and, in doing so, changed the world. That is possible for each and every one of us. We can change the world.

The Soul of the Universe "has been called the Universal Feminine or the Holy Womb of Nature, because It is receptive and creative (Holmes, 1938, p 96)." It "is never an entity, although It acts as though It were (Holmes, 1938, p 97)." Because of the Love and Goodness built into the fabric of the Soul of the Universe, Infinite Intelligence or God, it can feel like an entity. But, if it were, that would limit what it is. There is a warmth that we feel, like we would another person. But this Soul of the Universe, remains limitless, all embracing, all knowing, all creating through the directive of Love and Goodness.

Chapter 5: Body

"The word "body" as used in the Science of Mind means all objective manifestations of the invisible Principle of Life. The body is distinguished from the idea, in that the body is seen while the idea is invisible (Holmes, 1938, p 98)." Anything in physical form, which includes measurable energy, is body. Quantum physics uses the terms local and non-local. Local is defined as anything slower than the speed of light, which has been determined as the ultimate speed something can travel in the physical universe. Anything traveling faster than the speed of light is considered non-local. Thought is a non-local event, as it is instantaneous, thus traveling faster than the speed of light.

"The physical body is evolved for the purpose of allowing consciousness to function on this plane (Holmes, 1938, p 99)." There have been experiments conducted which have proven the existence of non-local communication between two local events. My favorite experiment is where two participants, after meditating on communication with each other for twenty minutes, are placed in separate Faraday rooms. These are rooms that do not allow any form of local matter or energy to penetrate their exterior. Both participants are attached to EEG machines, which measure brain wave activity. A strobe light set to random intervals, flashes in one of the participant's eyes, while that person's brain wave activity is measured. At the same moment, instantaneously, faster than the speed of light, the other participant, sitting in a room with no strobe, shows the same brain wave activity in almost equal strength. This can only be the case if the consciousness of one of the participants is communicating through the consciousness of the other participant to the other participant's body.

"The idea of body is an image derived from the fountain of all ideas (Holmes, 1938, p 100)." From this fountain of ideas springs forth all that appears in physical form. Every physical form is made out of the same Body, the same Soul and the same Spirit. "That which the Spirit involves must evolve (Holmes, 1938, p 100)!" Evolution must also be built into everything or evolution could not take place, except in random intervals that would not involve everything. But, evolution does involve everything as witnessed in the tiniest virus, as well as our greatest minds and ideas.

"We should then see... the world of multiplicity is deep-rooted in a Universe of Unity (Holmes, 1938, p 102)." Every thought, belief, feeling, or action; every bit of matter or energy in all its amazingly different, diverse and unique forms; evolves out of the limitless One we call Infinite Intelligence or God. "When the knowledge of this unity comes alike to all, the tread of armies will cease and the bugle call will echo the soft notes of brotherly love (Holmes, 1938, p 103)."

"The Universe as we see it is not even a fractional part of the Universe that actually is (Holmes, 1938, p 104)." There may be multiple universes or layers of universes that go on forever. Because we know this Infinite Intelligence to be limitless, we cannot know its boundaries because it doesn't have any. Any possibility we conceive must already exist in the One Mind. Any possibility yet to be conceived must also already exist in the One Mind. As we evolve, we gain an ever increasing perception of this limitlessness and thus gain an ever increasing ability to use it. What we manifest into physical form is wholly based on how large our mental picture can encompass the limitless possibilities. What we see and experience in Body is the message from our higher selves of exactly how large a mental picture we have at any given moment.

Chapter 6: [Our] Relationship to the Spiritual Universe

"Whatever is true of the Universe as a Whole must also be true of the individual as some part of this Whole. Man is evolved from the Universe as a self-conscious, thinking center of Living Spirit, and as such he must, in his nature and being, reproduce the Universe (Holmes, 1938, p 106)." One of my favorite analogies by Dr. Holmes is, "A single drop of water is not the whole ocean, but it does contain within itself the same qualities and attributes (Holmes, 1938, p 107)." Of course, this is based on the Rumi poem, "You are not just a drop in the ocean, but the entire ocean in a drop." We are the very essence of the Divine as a unique and magnificent expression of the One. We have within us the power of the universe to bring forth into the world anything that is ours to create.

Though we contain the Whole, we are individuals and each of us expresses our Divine nature in our unique way. Picasso didn't create as Van Gogh and Van Gogh didn't create as Picasso. It actually works that we don't open to all that is the Whole, but only that which is ours to grasp. Certainly, what we grasp can grow exponentially throughout our lives; however, if everyone expressed limitlessness there would be no uniqueness. Our individuality is what makes the world such a rich place. It is the miraculous orchestra of humanity, each a unique instrument, creating anew every moment, an ever evolving symphony for the ages.

"The Science of Mind and Spirit, makes a tremendous claim when it states that the individual should be free from the bondage of sickness, poverty and unhappiness. It does, however, carefully set forth the conditions under which freedom operates and the laws governing Life, stating in no uncertain terms that unless man understands these conditions and obeys these laws, he will not receive full benefit from its teachings (Holmes, 1938, p 107)." The laws of science show us how to create the internet, computers and rockets to the moon and beyond. If we don't follow and use these laws exactly as

29

prescribed, the internet, computers and rockets crash. It is the same with the Science of Mind. When we understand and use these laws in the way they work, we create a life that works, instead of a life that crashes. Just like the laws of science, these laws work whether we use them consciously or not. The difference in crashing or flying is not in whether the laws work, but in our understanding and in how we use them. "The Universe is fool-proof. It does say we can have what we can take, while at the same time we must expect to experience the logical result of our [embodiment], be it good or what we call evil (Holmes, 1938, p 110)."

"If man takes his images of thought only from his previous experiences, then he continues in the bondage which those previous experiences create. If we talk about discord, we shall become more discordant. The more the world arms for war, the more certain it is that there will be war. People who spend all their time talking about their unhappiness become more unhappy. Jesus understood these great laws of cause and effect in the Universe, which work sometimes with apparent slowness but always with sureness. Eventually we shall understand that all human bondage is an invention of ignorance (Holmes, 1938, p 110)."

The age-long discussion of the problem of evil will never be answered until we realize that evil is not a thing of itself. It is simply a misuse of the Law of Freedom (Holmes, 1938, p 111)." As we talked about in Part III of the Introduction, Love and Goodness are built into the fabric of the Universe. As we evolve, we recognize more and more the power of Love that is pervasive throughout our being. Because we have free will, we can create discord, if we so choose. There is nothing forcing us to do good except the gentle tugging of our own heart strings, which can be silenced only by ourselves, through great pain to ourselves.

To suppose that one must retire from the world to be spiritual is one of the greatest possible mistakes (Holmes, 1938, p 114)." The best way for us to know how much of the spiritual law we understand and use is by looking at what we have created in our lives and how close it is to what we want. We learn nothing of the creative process by sitting in a cave by ourselves. It is through our day to day interaction with the world that we uncover whatever it is we need to learn and heal about ourselves and the metaphysical laws that are at our disposal to create.

We can take that learning into a quiet space for prayer or meditation and significantly develop our skill in knowing the truth for ourselves and others. However, every experience we have is a spiritual experience. It is not that we go to a job, do all the things that need doing during the day and then take time in the evening or on weekends for our spiritual activity. Every activity is spiritual because every activity or experience we have is Spirit. "There is One Universal Substance whose business it is to take form in multiplicity (Holmes, 1938, p 116)." Whether that multiplicity is things or experiences, it all comes forth from Spirit, Infinite Intelligence, the Soul of the Universe, Subjective Mind, God, whatever you call it; *thus everything is spiritual.*

Not everything or every experience is self-aware. "IT IS ONE THING TO SAY THAT OUR FEET DO NOT KNOW THEY ARE FEET AND QUITE ANOTHER THING TO SAY THAT THEY ARE ILLUSIONS (Holmes, 1938, p 117)." A rock may not know it's a rock, but it still exists as a rock. For it to exist, consciousness, on some level, must have held the mental equivalent for that rock. But, the rock itself does not need to hold its own mental equivalent for it to exist. This is true of the many different parts of our bodies, as it is true for the many different parts of the Body of God, which we call the physical universe. For the universe and everything in it to exist, there must be a self-aware consciousness that held the mental equivalent for this physical universe. The truth of this exists in the Law we use as individuals, for what works for one works for all and must come out of the All that is Infinite. If humans alone had self-awareness, it would mean we had something the great Infinite did not have. That cannot be the case. Thus, the

Infinite Intelligence must be aware of Itself. Self-awareness exists. The self-awareness of Infinite Intelligence is large enough to create the physical universe and beyond. Our own self-awareness is as large as we can evolve it to be.

"[N]o matter what may be in the subjective state of our thought, the conscious state can change it; this is what treatment does (Holmes, 1938, p 118)." We can use this amazing power of self-awareness to hold a mental equivalent of any life we can imagine. That is the power of the Law. That is the power of the type of prayer we call treatment. "Whatever is held in consciousness until it becomes a part of the subjective side of thought, tends to take place in the world of affairs (Holmes, 1938, p 119)." As we have spoken of previously, our lives reflect the totality of what we embody. Any negative thoughts, feelings and beliefs, conscious and unconscious, as well as all the race consciousness thoughts, feelings and beliefs regarding whatever it is we want to create, affects the outcome.

Law works on the mathematical trend of our desires, not the individual thought. It is up to us to infuse our thoughts, feelings, beliefs and actions with a deep knowing that what we want already exists. It is through this deep knowing, or embodiment, that what we want already exists in the Mind of God, and so must exist in the Body of God, and so comes into physical form. Nothing—not our unconscious beliefs, nor race consciousness—are stronger than our knowing. Nothing is stronger than truly knowing, or embodying, the mental equivalent we see within, as already here.

"The Spirit of Christ means that [embodiment] which recognizes the Law and uses It for constructive purposes only. The spirit of Antichrist means the spirit of the individual who understanding the Law, uses It destructively (Holmes, 1938, p 120)." All we are really talking about here is the discord created when we silence our true nature and try to build a life without Love and Goodness. Because we have free will, it is, of course, possible to do so. However, in the same way that water can create great caverns and a grand canyon through a substance like rock, Love will ultimately crack a hardened heart. Even if it takes an entire lifetime or even many lifetimes, Love will win.

"Each individual maintains his identity in Law, through his personal use of Law, and each is drawing from Life what he [embodies] into it (Holmes, 1938, p 123)." Yet, "This is not done by holding thoughts, but by knowing the Truth. There is a vast difference, a difference which too few realize (Holmes, 1938, p 123)." Knowing is the key here. By knowing, we mean embodiment. Knowing is not a thought or idea. It's not a feeling or belief. As we have spoken of, knowing is the totality of who we are. We can say we know something, but that doesn't make it so. We can think we know something, when it's really intellectualized. When we really know it, that knowing is in our bones, in our bloodstream, beyond our mental faculties. We don't question what we know.

Guitarists experience this knowing when their fingers go to a place on the fretboard without them having to look at the fretboard or think about where their fingers are going. How they get to that point of knowing takes, for most, many hours of practice. It is the same with knowing the Truth. We start with many hours of stating the Truth, thinking the Truth and holding a mental equivalent of what we want in the Truth. With enough practice, this knowing is embodied. Because physical form is a perfect reflection of what we embody, the moment we embody the Truth, and the mental equivalent of what we want, what we want shows up in physical form.

The Truth is that *there is only One*. All is in the same Unity. "We arrive at a consciousness of Unity only in such degree as we see that what we are looking FOR, we are looking WITH, and looking AT (Holmes, 1938, p 124)." We can only experience Unity to the extent we can open our individual consciousness to the fact it exists. "..the student of metaphysics is learning to consciously control the stream of thought that he allows to enter his inner and creative mentality

(Holmes, 1938, p 125)." Our thoughts are the food of our beliefs. Our beliefs are the food of what we embody. What we embody is the food of our creation and what actually shows up in physical form. We can change what we experience in our lives because we can change our thoughts, which, if we practice enough, will change our beliefs, which will change what we embody and ultimately change our life experience.

"Someone may say, "I cannot imagine God not caring." I cannot either, but we are dealing with Law. "Does the law of electricity care whether it cooks the dinner or burns the house (Holmes, 1938, p 127)?" The Law must be impartial because we have free will and the ability to create. If It behaved in any other manner, we would not have free will to create.

Yet, we know there is a directive of Love and Goodness built into the fabric of everything, urging us to be loving and good. This is why every enlightened person becomes more compassionate. The more aware we become of the Divine, the more we feel ourselves as One with the All, the more loving and kind we become, because we feel and hear the gentle nudge and use our free will to choose to answer Its calling.

"When we know our Oneness with God and Law, what a great burden is removed. Any sense of opposition is removed from the consciousness which perceives Unity (Holmes, 1938, p 127)." "Everything comes from Intelligence. There is nothing but Unity; there is nothing but freedom; there is nothing but completeness; there is nothing but Totality (Holmes, 1938, p 128)." The more we understand this, the less discord we experience in our lives. The more we embody this, the more our lives become the magnificent, Divine experiences they were always meant to be. "Such is the power of right [embodiment] that it cancels and erases everything unlike itself. It answers every question, solves all problems, is the solution to every difficulty. It is like the Sunlight of Eternal Truth bursting through the clouds of obscurity and bathing all life in a celestial glory. It is the Absolute with which we are dealing and nothing less (Holmes, 1938, p 128)."

Chapter 7: Summary of Part One: The Nature of Being

"There is a Universal Presence that acts as though It were intelligent, and we may assume that It is. There is a Universal Intelligence acting as Law— we may also assume this to be true. There is a formless Stuff in the Universe, forever taking form, and forever changing its form— this we may accept as being self-evident. We have every reason to postulate a three-fold nature of the Universal Being, which we shall call Spirit, Soul, and Body. We shall think of Spirit as the great Actor, Soul as the Medium of Its action, and Body the result of Its action (Holmes, 1938, p 129)." This beautiful description of the nature of Being gives us an image we can use to take charge of creating our lives. We are working with the Principle that Infinite Intelligence or God, is self-aware; Universal Presence or Spirit. This self-awareness is individualized within each of us. Through our self-awareness we send out a message to this Infinite Intelligence; the Law or Soul. This message is the totality of our embodiment. The Infinite Intelligence brings into form out of the formless a reflection of the message we have sent out; Body. By understanding and learning how this three-fold nature works, we can use it in the same way we use electricity; for our good.

"Man discovers his ability to think and realizes that from within there comes a reaction to his thought. He can think consciously and mental law acts upon his thought; and his physical body is affected by his thinking. He next discovers that he can think for others, causing a corresponding action in and through their bodies. In this way, he discovers a mental medium through which thought operates. He now realizes himself to be a thinking center in a Universal Mind (Holmes, 1938, p 130)." This is why Licensed Practitioners can pray for others. As we have discussed, thinking is only the first step. Whosoever embodies a knowing of something the deepest, that is what will take physical form. So, if I have a knowing that houses sell easily and have demonstrated this knowing by selling my own house easily and someone comes to me who has doubt about their house selling and asks me to know for them that their house will, sell there is a very strong probability it will, because knowing trumps doubt every time.

"Soul and Universal Subjective Mind have the same meaning, and are the Creative Medium of all thought and action. Soul is also the Substance of Spirit, the unformed Stuff, from which all forms are evolved (Holmes, 1938, p 131)." "Creation is eternally going on; change is always taking place within that which is Changeless (Holmes, 1938, p 131)." We have an opportunity at every single point in our lives to make a change by changing what we embody. Until a change in thinking becomes knowing or embodiment, that change may not occur. It always starts with our thoughts. The more our thoughts rest in the knowing that what we want to see take form already exists, the more we impress that change of form in Universal Mind. Once we have fully embodied that change, Universal Mind reflects it into physical form.

"Spirit makes things out of Itself by becoming the thing It makes (Holmes, 1938, p 131)." Everything is the Thing Itself, so, of course, whatever shows up in physical form is the Thing Itself showing up as Itself. This is why we are such powerful beings. We are the Thing Itself; as we have already quoted Rumi as saying, "not just a drop, but the entire ocean in a drop."

"Man re-enacts the Divine Nature on all three planes. He is self-knowing in his conscious mind, creative through his subconscious reactions, and he has a body (Holmes, 1938, p 132)." There is only One. This One is the Word that creates, the formless Nature that all creations come into form out of, and the physical form itself. "[We have] at [our] disposal, in what [we] call… subjective mind, a power that is Limitless; this is because [we are] One with the Whole on the subjective side of Life (Holmes, 1938, p 133)." This is the ultimate Truth; we are this One Mind, only limited by our ability to grasp the Infinite nature of this One Mind. Yet, it's important to note that to create the life of our dreams, we do not need to grasp the

36

Infinite. We just need to grasp and embody enough of this Infinite Source that we are able to express ourselves in the world in a way that fulfills who we truly are; unique expressions of the Divine. No one else needs to paint like Van Gogh. He already did that. We just need to paint the life that we dream it to be. By embodying that dream and grasping Its reality as already done, we use this magnificent power of the Infinite Intelligence that we are and that dream comes into being.

"Man already has, within himself, the key to freedom but he must come to realize his relation to the Whole. This relationship is one of complete Unity (Holmes, 1938, p 134)." Every time we recognize a deeper sense of this Unity, we feel the Love and Goodness that is the basis of Infinite Intelligence. As we experience this Love and Goodness, we breathe easier, knowing this Infinite Intelligence is on our side; we are one with the One and we are free.

Chapter 8: The Power of Thought

"From the Bible we have the assurance: "As a man thinketh in his heart, so is he." The old Greek philosophers understood something of the meaning of thought. What we expect, said Aristotle, that we find. What we wish, said Demosthenes, that we believe. And Shakespeare is accredited with the saying: "There is nothing either good or bad but thinking makes it so." It is one thing to know a principle, another to apply it (Holmes, 1938, p 137)." There are thousands upon thousands of anecdotes about people who have healed themselves through believing it to be so. The medical community believes so strongly in the effect of placebos it has to be included in any real testing of a product to see if the results from using the product are different from the results of the placebo. There have been studies on the power of prayer, even when the person being prayed for was unaware, that have shown extraordinary results. There is no doubt to the power of thought, and yet, when we do doubt, a doubting thought has power, too. Our doubts weigh in just as strongly to what we embody as any other thoughts. Weeding those out can create a powerful knowing.

"The possibility of healing physical disease, changing environment, attracting friends and demonstrating supply through the power of right thinking, rests entirely on the theory that we are… Infinite Mind, which reacts to our [embodiment] according to Law (Holmes, 1938, p 138)." This is the "as me" point of view I spoke about in my introduction to this book. Infinite Mind doesn't just flow through us. We are Infinite Mind. Our lives reflect back to us the perfect mirror of what we embody whether we believe that it does or not. The more we can understand and embrace this most powerful principle, the more we can weed out from within what does not serve us and embody what does. The more we embody healing, supply, friends and the environment we wish to live in, the more they show up in physical form.

"As individual intelligence, we communicate with each other— are able to respond to each other— and in so doing we establish the fact that intelligence responds to intelligence. This same law must hold good, whether we think of finite intelligence responding to finite intelligence, or Infinite Intelligence responding to finite intelligence— for intelligence is the same in ESSENCE wherever we find it (Holmes, 1938, p 138)." "Whatever intelligence we possess is some degree of the One Intelligence, which we call God (Holmes, 1938, p 139)." To whatever degree we grasp ourselves as the One Intelligence is still the whole. We are not missing a piece of the Infinite Intelligence. It isn't hiding from us. It is not out of our reach. The entirety is available to us all the time. To the extent each of us believes we can access this Infinite Intelligence, that is the extent of our embodiment and *what we embody manifests*.

"We are immersed in an Infinite Creative Medium which, because of Its Nature, must create after the pattern our thought gives It (Holmes, 1938, p 140)." This Infinite Intelligence, we call God, is creating all the time. It is Its nature to create. It is our nature to create. Thus, we are creating all the time, too. But, "Our beliefs and our deep-seated convictions inevitably out-picture and reflect themselves in our experience and environment, both in the physical condition of the body, and in the larger world of our affairs (Holmes, 1938, p 140)." So, in the end, our thoughts are just the beginning point. It is important to train our thinking, because our thinking feeds our beliefs. It is important to uncover our deep-seated beliefs and make sure that they are in line with what we want to create, because our beliefs feed what we embody. And most important:ly It is what we embody that comes into form every minute of every day. Sometimes we can shift what we embody instantaneously. Sometimes, it takes time. But, because Infinite Intelligence is creating all the time, we are creating what we embody, just like we create anything else. As we create what we embody to be what we want to out-picture, that out-picturing is the form that takes shape in our lives. "Realizing, then, that while the Power is limitless, It must become operative through our own [embodiment], we shall see that what we need is not some greater power, but a greater consciousness, a deeper realization of life, a more sublime concept of Being, a more intimate concept of an already indwelling God, Who is personal to us by virtue of being personified [as] us (Holmes, 1938, p 141)."

"The movement of consciousness upon itself creates a motion or vibration upon Substance, the force of which is equal to the embodiment of the thought set in motion (Holmes, 1938, p 141)." This is why thinking something once rarely produces the desired result. It is the depths of who we are that we are talking about here. Our minds, hearts and bodies expressing a totality that is up to us to bring into alignment. It is whatever alignment we are expressing as a totality, whether for our conscious desires, or against our conscious desires, that is actually showing up in the world. "We are all immersed in the atmosphere of our own thinking, which is the direct result of all we have ever said, thought or done (Holmes, 1938, p 142)." So, you can see the importance of being clear on what the totality, or what you embody, is expressing into the Infinite Intelligence which is then taking form in your life. "When we understand the Law, we learn to consciously embody what we wish, and think of this only, and then we are drawn silently toward it (Holmes, 1938, p 142)." Our desires take form at the exact moment we fully embody that form within us. Not a second sooner or later. In this way we can know exactly what we have embodied by what we have in form. The beauty of all this is "That which thought has done, thought can un-do (Holmes, 1938, p 142)."

"Consciousness in this sense means an inner embodiment of ideas. If one wishes to demonstrate prosperity, he must first have a consciousness of prosperity; if he wishes health, he must embody the idea of health (Holmes, 1938, p 143)." There is a saying that goes, "simple, but not easy." That is what we are facing here. The simplicity is this: *what we embody manifests*. The not-so-easy part is how we must discipline our thinking to feed our consciousness and ultimately, embody what we desire to grow. "Every day, every moment, every second, there is choice (Holmes, 1938, p 143)." The best way to bring into form what we desire is to use as many moments as possible to choose the thoughts we want to embody, instead of allowing our unconscious thoughts to be what we embody.

If we don't understand the effect on our embodiment and, thus, on what we have created in our lives, from all that is unconscious in us, it is easy to fall into the idea that we are victimized by something external or out of our control. It is through this understanding that we can gain the discipline to empower ourselves and shape the lives of our dreams. "There is One Infinite Principle, One Infinite Thought-Stuff, One Infinite Creative Power, but countless numbers of forms, which change as the specific idea behind them changes (Holmes, 1938, p 144)."

"[W]e do assert that a prolonged discordant mental state is certain to eventuate in some form of physical ailment. People have died of great grief; of broken hearts; of outbursts of temper; of deep and continued resentment; of excessive worry, and many other mental states, in which there was no specific thought of sickness at all. The point to remember is, that all mind activity inevitably tends to create its physical correspondent (Holmes, 1938, p 145)." Unhealthy thoughts of any sort, lead to feeding unhealthy beliefs, which feed an unhealthy embodiment, so, of course, that leads to unhealthy physical forms; within and without our bodies. "If any word has power, it follows that all words have power (Holmes, 1938, p 146)." This is an incredibly important point to remember. It is not just prayer or spiritual mind treatment that feeds our embodiment, and thus, Infinite Intelligence, with what we want to create. We are feeding what manifests in our lives every single moment with every thought we think. "God's Creative Power of Mind is right here. We have as much of this power to use as we believe in and embody (Holmes, 1938, p 146)." The larger our understanding, acceptance and embodiment of this immense power at our command, the better we can use it consciously.

The Love and Goodness that is the essence of God's Creative Power is nudging us all the time; but, because we have free will, it is up to each of us to listen and allow that Love and Goodness to fill our conscious awareness. Love is a choice. Though it is within the very fabric of who we are, our free will allows us to choose as discordant a life as we want. It is up to us to embrace and embody our true nature; Love. "The Prodigal Son remained a prodigal as long as he chose to do so. When he chose to, he returned to his "Father's house" and was greeted with outstretched hands. So shall our experience be when we return to the world which is perfect; there will be something that will turn to us (Holmes, 1938, p 147)."

"We have gone far in the right direction, when we have determined that Creation could have originated only in Intelligence; and have realized further that our own mental power must be the same in kind with the Creativeness of God (Holmes, 1938, p 148)." There is only One. One light, one love, one healing, loving source. Because there is only One, we must be this One. There is nothing outside this Infinite Intelligence, so our intelligence must be this Infinite Intelligence, too. These are the first two steps of what we call Spiritual Mind Treatment. We first recognize that there is only One Infinite Presence, there is only One Mind and that must mean that we are this One Mind, too. It must be the case as there is nothing else we could be.

There are those who say the first two steps of treatment are all you need. They say once we have truly embodied that we are this Oneness, all is available to us instantly and eternally. They are speaking of an "as me" embodiment. When we embody "As me", our word, would, of course, express instantly. Then we would experience the Power of Thought as the ever-flowing creative force it most certainly is. They might be right. It is for each of us to discover and uncover for ourselves.

43

Chapter 9: Prayer

"One of the questions most frequently asked about the Science of Mind is, "Are prayers and treatments identical?" The answer to this question is both Yes and No. If when one prays his prayer is a recognition of Spirit's Omniscience, Omnipotence, and Omnipresence, and a realization of man's unity with Spirit, then his prayer is a spiritual treatment.

If, on the other hand, one is holding to the viewpoint that God is some far off Being, whom he would approach with doubt in his thought; wondering if by some good luck he may be able to placate God or persuade Him of the wisdom of one's request— then, there is but little similarity between prayer and treatment. Nothing could bring greater discouragement than to labor under the delusion that God is a Being of moods, who might answer some prayers and not others (Holmes, 1938, p 149)."

Spiritual Mind treatment is an active prayer, an affirmative prayer, meant to deepen our embodiment of our Oneness with the One Mind—the Infinite Intelligence. When done correctly, there is no sense of separateness as if praying to a being outside ourselves. Instead, we feel the presence of this Infinite Intelligence as ourselves, as the cells of our very being, as the nature of our personal Soul. "The secret of spiritual power lies in a consciousness of one's union with the Whole, and of the availability of Good (Holmes, 1938, p 151)."

The deeper we embody the principles of Love, Peace, Harmony, Power, Wisdom, Wholeness and Abundance that we intuitively know express what this Oneness is, the more these principles express in our lives. "If one makes himself receptive to the idea of love, he becomes lovable. To the degree that he embodies love, he is love; so people who love are loved (Holmes, 1938, p 151)." It is up to us to weed out that which does not serve us, yet, until we put a stop to it, it proliferates within us. We, then feed ourselves thoughts that we want to embody and thus express and through expression, create. Prayer, especially the type of prayer we call Spiritual Mind Treatment, is a wonderful vehicle for feeding ourselves thoughts we want to embody and shifting within to create the desired result without.

"Through [treatment] we recognize a spiritual law, that has always existed... (Holmes, 1938, p 152)." By recognizing this spiritual law, through treatment, we bring to light a power that has been creating our lives through our unconscious embodiment and gives us the possibility of creating consciously. "As fire warms the body, as food strengthens us, as sunshine raises our spirits, so there is a subtle transfusion of some invisible force in such communion, weaving itself into the very warp and woof of our own mentalities (Holmes, 1938, p 152)." This is the power of Spiritual Mind Treatment.

"So we learn to go deeply within ourselves, and speak as though there were a Presence there that knows; and we should take the time to unearth this hidden cause, to penetrate this inner chamber of consciousness. It is most worthwhile to commune with Spirit— to sense and feel It. The approach to Spirit is direct... through our own consciousness (Holmes, 1938, p 153)." Spiritual Mind Treatment is a prayer of letting go of separation. We step beyond the veil of what we have labeled as reality into the true realm of creation. We see our lives and the lives of everyone in the context of a greater whole. We feel the directive of Love and Goodness gently tugging us towards its fruition, through us and as us. We remind ourselves that, of course, what we embody takes form in our lives. We affirm that which must already exist in the limitless nature of the One to be in form here and now. We express the Truth and we know it to be so.

"Every day and every hour we are meeting the eternal realities of life, and in such degree as we co-operate with these eternal realities in love, in peace, in wisdom, and in joy— believing and receiving— we are automatically blessed (Holmes, 1938, p 154)." The more we pray in this manner, the deeper we embody the essence of Unity and Love, until we have aligned ourselves with Principle to the point where, "Our prayer is answered before it is uttered (Holmes, 1938, p 154)."

Chapter 10: Faith

"Faith has been recognized as a power throughout the ages —whether it be faith in God, faith in one's fellow [human beings], in oneself, or in what one is doing... Those who have great faith, have great power (Holmes, 1938, p 155)." This, again, is the heart of our teaching. To the extent we have faith, or embodiment, in how the creative power of Infinite Intelligence works and that we are this Infinite Intelligence uniquely expressing Itself as us, we create our lives consciously. To the extent that we have faith in the Goodness built into the fabric of life, that Goodness shows up in our lives. To the extent that we have faith in humanity, ourselves and in what we are doing, we will experience each accordingly.

"But what is fear? Nothing more nor less than the negative use of faith... faith misplaced (Holmes, 1938, p 156)." Remembering that every thought is a prayer and imprints itself into the Law, fear is faith that something will go badly and that faith has as much power as the faith in something going well. This is what makes it so important to grab a hold of ourselves when we are afraid and refocus our thoughts to what it is we want instead of what scares us. ""Faith is ... the evidence of things not seen (Holmes, 1938, p 156)." So, whether we hold our thoughts in the good or the fear, it's still faith. "When we use our creative imagination in strong faith, it will create for us, out of the One Substance, whatever we have [embodied] (Holmes, 1938, p 157)."

Our imagination has great creative power. We can imagine the worst or we can imagine the best. It is up to us. Whatever we choose to imagine, that is what we have faith in. But, we, who believe that there is only One and that this One is a source of good, know that "[i]f the good were not already ours in the invisible supply, it would be impossible for us to procure it in any manner (Holmes, 1938, p 157)." It is our faith, our deep knowing, in this One that allows us to find comfort in times of trouble, know we are not alone, and gives us the confidence that what we pronounce and embody shows up in physical form in our lives. "The Universe exists by Its own self-pronouncement, by Its own affirmation. It only knows "I AM." It knows nothing else (Holmes, 1938, p 157)."

"Persons familiar with Biblical history hardly need a lesson about faith, for the eleventh chapter of Hebrews is full of instances proving its sustaining power. Paul enumerates at length the experiences of Enoch, Noah, Abraham, Moses, Gideon, Samuel and the prophets, and many more, "who through faith subdued kingdoms, wrought righteousness, obtained promises, stopped the mouths of lions, quenched the power of fire, escaped the edge of the sword; out of weakness were made strong, waxed mighty in power, turned to flight armies of aliens, women received their dead raised to life again."

Our ancestors believed these records and embodied this living faith in their consciousness, thereby leaving us a great legacy. Whatever they did, they were able to do because they held to an unwavering faith in the Power of the One and they were this One. "Since Faith is a quality unconfined to age or station, it may be ours today as much as it has been any man's at any time (Holmes, 1938, p 158)." Remembering that faith is expressing itself through us consciously or unconsciously, these Bible stories represent the best of conscious faith. Through the ages, those who took hold of their fear and knew the Truth of who they were changed history. Anyone of us can do that. Anyone of us, at any time can embody the faith we need to create the life of our dreams. "If one will have faith in himself, faith in his fellowmen, in the Universe, and in God, that faith will light the place in which he finds himself, and by the light of this faith, he will be able to see that ALL IS GOOD (Holmes, 1938, p 158)."

"Faith is built up from belief, acceptance and trust (Holmes, 1938, p 159)." The deeper we can trust that our lives work, the more the depth of that trust takes form in our lives. "We must know that we know (Holmes, 1938, p 159)."

"If we believe that the Spirit, incarnated in us, can demonstrate, shall we be disturbed at what appears to contradict this (Holmes, 1938, p 159)?" It is through our faith that we recognize, that no matter what a circumstance may look like, it must turn out for our good; that it *is already* for our good. As our faith builds, so does our confidence and our ability to relax when circumstances arise we may not like. Faith is what carries us through the rough times. "By spiritual understanding, is not meant anything strange or unnatural, but merely that the belief in goodness must be greater than any apparent manifestation of its opposite (Holmes, 1938, p 160)."

"It is wonderful to contemplate the [embodiment] of people who are not afraid to believe their prayers will be answered, and are not afraid to say, "I know." We shall all arrive at this same assurance, this perfect faith, in such degree as we cease contemplating the Universe as opposed to Itself (Holmes, 1938, p 161)." How can that which created the stars, earth, moon and every living being on this planet have any trouble at all creating whatever is your heart's desire? Faith is the key that unlocks the endless possibilities that are available to us every moment of every day. "Ours is the privilege of giving birth to the unborn possibility of limitless experience (Holmes, 1938, p 161)."

When "we fail to realize that Principle is not bound by precedent, we limit our faith to that which has already been accomplished, and few "miracles" result (Holmes, 1938, p 162)." When we stand in the faith that this moment is a creative moment filled with every possibility that ever was and ever will be our lives open in ways we never imagined and miracles become an everyday occurrence. "No matter what the outside appearance, we must cling steadfastly to the knowledge that God is good, and God is all (Holmes, 1938, p 162)." When we "cling steadfastly" in faith to the Truth, what others call miracles, for us is simply the logical outcome of prayer.

Chapter 11: Mental and Spiritual Treatment

"Effective mental treatment is propelled by a consciousness of love and a realization that the Creative Spirit is always at work. The practitioner does not feel that he must compel the Force to work. It is the nature of the Creative Power to take form, and it is the nature of man to use It. A treatment should be given in a calm, expectant manner and with a deep inner conviction of its reality, without any fear or any sense that the human mind must make it effective. The work is effective because the Law is always in operation (Holmes, 1938, p 163)." This speaks to the difference between "by me" and "as me" as I discussed in my introduction.

When we are in "by me" state of consciousness, we feel it is up to us to do the work, take the action, and make it happen. We are using our will to make whatever it is come into form. In an "as me" state of consciousness, we know ourselves and everything to be God. We recognize ourselves as the "Creative Spirit" at work. As practitioners, we must know deep down to our core, through any belief to the contrary, that what we want to manifest has already manifested in the One Mind, so, of course, shows up in physical form in our lives. Because we have free will, we can force stuff to show up, which, for some, is the only state of consciousness they know. In the forcing, we are embodying the need to force, creating a tougher and tougher dynamic that we then face in the world.

Through the development of an "as me" state of consciousness, we perceive the malleability of our reality, which, in turn, develops a dynamic of synchronicity and a flow with life and the world. We gain a trust in perfect and right time and relax into the perfection that is our lives.

"Treatment should incorporate a conscious recognition that health has always been ours, abundance has always been ours, happiness and peace have always been ours; they are ours now, for they are the very essence and Truth of our being

(Holmes, 1938, p 164)." The deeper the embodiment of Truth, the quicker the form appears. "We already live in a Perfect Universe, but It needs to be [embodied] before It can become a part of our experience (Holmes, 1938, p 164)." Through treatment, we allow ourselves to relax into the knowing that there is only One, which is perfect and complete. Like immersing ourselves in a hot bath, we rest in the comfort of the Divine. From this perspective, we embrace the Truth for ourselves, and, because there is no separation, for anyone else who has asked for treatment.

"[U]nless we realize… that as we deal with our own individuality, we are dealing with the Universal, which has projected out of Itself that which is like Itself on a miniature scale… unless we have this understanding, we shall be working much of the time on a basis of blind faith (Holmes, 1938, p 165)." Blind faith, though better than no faith at all, is not the same as embodiment. It is one of the most important lessons to learn about the creative process. Once again, I reiterate, we do not create by what we think, though, what we think feeds our beliefs. We do not create by what we believe, though what we believe feeds what we embody. In the end, we create what we embody. The physical form we experience in this world is the totality of what we have embodied reflected back to us every moment of every day. No matter what we tell ourselves about what we embody, it is easy to know what we embody by looking at what we actually are experiencing.

When a practitioner treats for another person, it's not about sending thoughts or suggestions. Everything takes place in the embodiment of the practitioner and, because there is only One Mind, embodies this same Truth for the person who asked for treatment. "If [the person requesting treatment] is receptive to the harmony of the belief which the practitioner has poured into Subjective Mind, it will externalize for [that person] at the level of the embodiment of the thought of the practitioner (Holmes, 1938, p 165)." So, when you are having trouble embodying a Truth for yourself, that is the perfect time to seek out a Licensed Practitioner. But, not just any Practitioner. Find one that has already demonstrated the same Truth you want for yourself. Because there is only One Mind, one person embodying the Truth can, without any strain or force, hold that Truth for anyone else, anywhere.

"The ones[s] who attempt... to heal [themselves] or another through a recognition of the creative power of Mind and the ever availability of Good, [are] mental or spiritual practitioner[s] (Holmes, 1938, p 167)." "The professional mental and spiritual practitioner is one who has dedicated [one's] life— [one's] time, ... energies, [and] intelligence— to helping others, through mental and spiritual means and methods (Holmes, 1938, p 168)." For those who think all we are talking about here is positive thinking, they do not understand how hard a Licensed Practitioner works to achieve the level of embodiment that not only brings to form a miraculous life for themselves, but for anyone who asks.

"The first requisite for the mental and spiritual practitioner is a full sense of the sacredness of... trust; [and] the sacredness of the confidence of the... patient... This confidence, a practitioner should keep sacred, inviolate (Holmes, 1938, p 168)." A Licensed Practitioner must be able to create a container of safety and love for the person asking for treatment. This means the practitioner's first job, before working with a client, is to make sure their own consciousness is clear of any doubt or discord. As we have said, it takes embodiment to bring whatever we want into form. Thus, a Practitioner must have this embodiment before they treat for anyone else for the Practitioner's treatment to be effective. The client need only be receptive. Everything happens in the mind of the Practitioner, which, of course is the One Mind, as is the client's. When the Practitioner knows, without a doubt, that what the client wants is already in physical form, and the client is receptive to this knowing, whatever is being treated for will, of course, take physical form.

"A scientific treatment cannot be conditioned upon anything that now exists, upon any experience less than perfection (Holmes, 1938, p 169)." We do not fix what is already in form. Every moment we are either recreating what already exists or creating something new. Every moment creation is occurring. The Practitioner does not treat to heal the sick or fix the broken. Whatever has form presently, has only as much effect on what has form in the next moment as we embody. This is proven time after time by the disappearance of tumors that were present a moment earlier, or, how, in an instant, life can go from feeling like you're sliding down into an endless pit, into enjoying the most amazing experience ever.

The anecdotes which express these experiences are countless. There is not a God up on a cloud deciding who gets to have a miracle and who doesn't. It is within each of us to create our own miracles. When we don't have the wherewithal to create for ourselves, then it is the time to reach out to a Licensed Practitioner who has demonstrated they can hold that embodiment for us, until we can hold it for ourselves.

"The more completely the practitioner is convinced of the power of [his or her] own word, the more power [that] word will have. THERE MUST BE A RECOGNITION THAT THE POWER OF THE WORD, OPERATING AS THE TRUTH AND REALITY OF BEING, CAN DO ALL THINGS. Therefore, the person whose consciousness is the clearest, who has the most complete faith, will be the best healer (Holmes, 1938, p 170)." When deciding on which Licensed Practitioner to treat for you, don't be afraid to ask about their lives. How a Practitioner's life is demonstrating is the best way to know in what areas their consciousness is clear and what areas they still have their own work to do. Always look for the one whose life has demonstrated in the area in which you want treatment.

"[T]here are but two distinct methods [of treatment]; one is called the argumentative and the other realization (Holmes, 1938, p 170)." In the argumentative method, we convince ourselves, step by step, that what we perceive is not the Truth and then commit to embodying what is the Truth until it takes

54

form. In the realization method, we simply know the Truth and do not address the current experience at all.

"The argumentative method... is a process of mental reasoning in which the practitioner argues to [him or herself] about [the] patient. [The practitioner] is presenting a logical argument to Universal Mind, or Principle, and if it carries with it complete evidence in favor of [the] patient, the patient should be healed (Holmes, 1938, p 170)." "The realization method is one whereby the practitioner realizes within [him or herself]— without the necessity of step by step building up a conclusion— the perfect state of [the] patient (Holmes, 1938, p 170)." Either one can be just as effective as the other. They both can reach the same conclusion. "Treatment is for the purpose of inducing an inner realization of perfection [embodied by] the practitioner, which inner realization, acting through Mind, operates through the patient (Holmes, 1938, p 170)." As long as the inner realization is embodied, the method used, argumentative or realization, is inconsequential.

The reason a Practitioner can treat for another person is simply "a thing which is known by any part of Universal Mind is known by every part of It, for It is an undivided Whole (Holmes, 1938, p 172)." The reason there are two methods is that not everyone uses their left and right brain the same. No matter which part of your brain is most dominant, there is still a method to treat effectively. "One method is a logical argument in the mind of the practitioner, by which [the practitioner] convinces [him or herself] of the Truth of Being; the other is the instant cutting through of all appearances to the Reality back of all things (Holmes, 1938, p 173)."

"As Jesus said, "Heaven and earth shall pass away, but my words shall not pass away." This is conviction, and if a practitioner does not have such conviction he must acquire it (Holmes, 1938, p 173)" before treating for others.

"Treatment has nothing to do with any effort which attempts to concentrate the Energy of God. The Energy of God is already concentrated everywhere. The gardener does not will potatoes and cabbages into being, but he has a willingness to comply with the law of nature, and provides the conditions which make it possible for this law to produce them (Holmes, 1938, p 174)." A Practitioner is the gardener of the One Mind, planting the seeds of embodiment for themselves and their clients, knowing that, of course, what they embody will come into physical form.

"We cannot demonstrate beyond our ability to... embody an idea (Holmes, 1938, p 174)." So it is that a Practitioner might be brilliant at creating abundance, but has health issues. Or, a Practitioner might have incredible health and well being, but struggle with finding the perfect job. "The possibility of demonstrating does not depend upon environment, condition, location, personality or opportunity (Holmes, 1938, p 174)." The depth of acceptance of this fact, combined with the embodiment of the form the client wants manifested, speaks to whether or not that particular form will manifest. Again, this knowing must be in the Practitioner. The client need only be receptive.

Because we are not treating to change the current condition, but to create anew in the current moment, we do not deny the condition that is present. "To claim that [a client] is perfectly normal, while the blood pressure remains high, would be to affront the intelligence of any sane individual (Holmes, 1938, p 175)." "Let us not deceive ourselves about our treatments (Holmes, 1938, p 176)." It is when we behave as if the current condition doesn't exist that we send a message about what we believe that is untrue. The same delusional message is present if we believe positive thinking will change anything all by itself. What the Practitioner does is very real and extremely effective. Unhealthy conditions exist just the same as healthy ones. Anything exists in the One Mind and can take physical form as easily as anything else. It is because there is only One Mind, one Infinite Intelligence that, just as easily as anything can take form, another form can come into

56

being, instantaneously, that is much closer or exactly what it is we want.

If a practitioner is using the argumentative method, then he or she will walk through the current conditions and see beyond them to the Truth of what's possible. This doesn't deny the current condition, but embraces that at any given moment, we can create anew. What existed a moment before can transform instantly once the new form desired is embodied.

Using the realization method, the present condition is not addressed at all. It is not denied or argued against. The Practitioner simply embodies the new form which the client wants to manifest and through the practitioner's embodiment, the Law reflects back that which has been embodied into physical form. "The only secret is the persistent ability to use the Law, and the determination to continue to use It until we prove It (Holmes, 1938, p 176)."

Chapter 12: Summary of Part Two: Spiritual Mind Healing

"The possibility of spiritual mind healing, changing environment, controlling conditions, etc., through the power of [embodiment], rests entirely upon the theory that we are surrounded by a Universal Mind, which reacts to [what we embody]— and always according to Law. Spiritual [Humanity] is Perfect, but [our] individual use of Life and Law enables [us] to cover a perfect idea with an apparently imperfect cloak (Holmes, 1938, p 177)." This, once again, speaks to how each of us individualizes the One Mind. Our personalities, beliefs, ideas, thoughts and embodiment, along with all we've taken in from race consciousness, make up what we put forth into the Law, and thus, what is created in our lives. We wear the totality of what we embody, cloaking the brilliant light of the One, the same way we wear clothes that cover our bodies.

This is a beautiful Principle. Each one of us is showing up as the One in our own unique way. I love the way Dr. Holmes uses the words "apparently imperfect", because it is we who judge what is perfect or not. It is our perception of the apparent imperfection that gives it weight. Each of us is actually a magnificent gift of the One in the form we have taken. Here, I reiterate the poet, Rumi, describing the wholeness we truly are. He says, "You are not a drop in the ocean. You are the entire ocean in a drop."

"Prayer is essential to the conscious well-being of the soul (Holmes, 1938, p 178)." Through prayer we develop the Faith we need to rest in the Truth. True "Faith is based on Immutable Principle (Holmes, 1938, p 178)." Because we know that everything is of the One Mind, or "Immutable Principle", "A mental treatment [or prayer] begins and ends within the [embodiment] of the practitioner, because [the practitioner] is in the same Mind in which [the] patient lives (Holmes, 1938, p 178)." "A practitioner does not try to suggest, hypnotize or mentally influence; [the practitioner] simply seeks to know that the client is now a spiritual being, and... holds to that belief no matter what the appearance may be. Right mental treatment does not tire the one giving the treatment (Holmes, 1938, p 179)." This is an important point. Spiritual Mind Treatment is not an act of will. No exertion should take place. It is a knowing; an embodiment of the

Truth for the one being treated. The Practitioner simply meditates or prays as many times as is necessary to reach such a state of embodiment that, of course, whatever is being treated for shows up in physical form.

"Healing is not a process but a revelation; for the revealing of the perfect [person] always heals (Holmes, 1938, p 179)." Herein this statement is one of the great paradoxes of enlightenment. The more we heal through revealing the perfect person that is the One, the more our unique expression of the One shines brilliantly. The more we embody the Unity of the Universal Mind, the greater our individualized use of the Law becomes manifest in our personal lives.

There are those who speak of dropping the ego and yet the ego is what makes us who we are. We can be the perfect person and be our amazing individual selves at the same time. "The greatest good that can come to anyone is the forming within him of an absolute certainty of himself, and of his relationship to the Universe, forever removing the sense of heaven as being outside himself. Such an understanding teaches us that there can never come a time when we shall stop progressing; that age is an illusion, that limitation is a mistake, that unhappiness is ignorance. This understanding will rob man of his loneliness and give him a sense of security which knows no fear, a peace without which no life can be happy, a poise which is founded on this peace, and a power which is the result of the union of peace with poise (Holmes, 1938, p 180)."

Chapter 13: Causes and Conditions

"The philosophy of spiritual mind healing is based upon the conception that we are living in a universe of Intelligence— a spiritual Universe; that thoughts are things, that definite states of consciousness, as they become subjective, operate through a creative field and tend to reproduce themselves in form. Therefore, it logically follows that this system of treatment is for the purpose of uncovering and neutralizing the wrong states of thought ... of building... a concept of our spiritual birthright. [Embodiment] which is built upon a realization of the Divine Presence has the power to neutralize negative thought, to erase it, just as light has the power to overcome darkness; not by combating darkness, but by being exactly what it is: LIGHT (Holmes, 1938, p183)." By neutralizing our negative thoughts and beliefs, we build "a concept of our spiritual birthright," that we are powerful, creative, spiritual beings and our lives work. This is not something we have to earn or prove to ourselves to receive, though many act as if that were so. We were born perfect spiritual beings. Whatever caused our negative concepts of ourselves is irrelevant and doesn't change the fact of who we truly are. With the use of spiritual mind healing we turn on the light and remember the Truth that has always been and always will be.

"Spirit is never bound by the form It takes, and is not affected by any apparent cause or condition, but is forever free (Holmes, 1938, p184)." It is simply that we may have forgotten our freedom. What we are doing through spiritual mind treatment is turning on the light to remember. "One, alone, in consciousness with the Infinite, constitutes a complete majority (Holmes, 1938, p184)." We have it all, everything we need, to create the life we desire. Our spirit is never bound by our present circumstances no matter what the form. "We must seek to realize the spiritual Universe, regardless of any condition which appears, if we would embody the greatest good (Holmes, 1938, p184)."

"To daily meditate on the Perfect Life, and to daily embody the Great Ideal, is a royal road to freedom, to that "peace which passeth understanding," and is happiness to the soul of man (Holmes, 1938, p185)." Practice, practice, practice. Like any skill, the more we practice spiritual mind treatment, the more we master that skill. The more we master, the more we embody the true Essence of who we are and create the life we want.

"Thinking of [any] weakness keeps the image of it before [us]. We cannot be too insistent on this all-important point: in treating, we must TURN ENTIRELY AWAY FROM THE CONDITION (Holmes, 1938, p185)." To clarify this point, we are not talking about denying the condition exits. It is that we must focus on the Spiritual Perfection, embodying and holding the image of that Truth instead of focusing on the condition. The more we can focus on the Truth, the more the condition must dissipate and change form. Where we focus is where our power goes. "The proper kind of a denial is based upon the recognition that, in reality, there is no limitation, for Mind can as easily make a planet as an acorn (Holmes, 1938, p186)." The "proper kind of denial" is that, whatever the condition , it has no power over our lives. It is to focus on where the true power exists, within the One Mind.

"Never limit your view of life by any past experience (Holmes, 1938, p187)." The only real moment is now. The only thing that makes the past persist is us. "The way scientifically to work out a problem is daily… to conceive of it as already being an accomplished fact in experience (Holmes, 1938, p187)." Time is only a continuum if we believe it as such. Every moment, every possibility exists in the here and now. When we hold the finished form as already done, we put the powerful force of the One Mind into action. "OUT OF ANY CHAOS WE CAN PRODUCE HARMONY (Holmes, 1938, p187)." It is within us to move mountains. It is up to us to believe and embody that this is so. "KNOW— without a shadow of doubt— that as a result of your treatment, some action takes place in Infinite Mind (Holmes, 1938, p188)." This is the key to everything talked about in this book, knowing-without a doubt. Everything hinges on how deeply we can embody who we truly are and what we can accomplish. Not only by our actions, but by our conscious knowing.

"The one practicing must be able to look a fact in the face, and know that all manifestations are effects and can be changed by changing the... cause. [We] must be able to look at the sick... , and know that only perfection stands before [us]; [we] must see beyond the appearance to that which is basically perfect (Holmes, 1938, p189)." Again, we are not denying that the condition is in physical form. We, as practitioners, must look beyond the form and see the Perfect Spirit from which the condition took form; from which all conditions take form. Every condition is made out of the same Perfect Spirit, taking physical form as a reflection of whatever we have embodied in that moment. As such, it is completely changeable and we are free to create our lives anew in any moment. "We must know that Truth produces freedom because Truth is freedom. Our work will best be done in quiet expectancy and in calm confidence. The results rest in the Eternal Law of Good (Holmes, 1938, p189)."

Chapter 14: Physical Perfection

"There is no question that people throughout the ages have been healed through prayer and faith (Holmes, 1938, p 190)," however, "Some prayers fall short of this state, while others reach a state of spiritual awareness. We come to understand, then, that the answer to prayer is in the prayer when it is prayed— the belief of the one praying sets in motion the Law of Love, which is the fundamental Law of the Universe (Holmes, 1938, p 190)." There is no outside God making decisions as to which prayer to answer. The depth of our embodiment is what makes all the difference. The Law is dispassionate and allows for free will. This is very important to understand. We are the reason some of our prayers are answered and some are not; but not because we are good or bad. There is no judgement in the One Mind. Beyond our conscious awareness is a world of unconscious thoughts, beliefs, and feelings feeding the totality of what we embody. It's like the underside of an iceberg, which is actually the larger knowing affecting our prayers.

"[T]o the degree in which we are able to see a perfect [person], [that perfect person] will appear (Holmes, 1938, p 191)." When the underside of the iceberg of our consciousness is in alignment with the upper side choice we want to create, then we have fully embodied our choice and that choice will appear in physical form. "Man will deliver himself from sickness and trouble in exact proportion to his discovery of himself and his true relationship to the Whole (Holmes, 1938, p 191)."
"We believe in every church and in all forms of worship. Above all, we certainly believe in God (Holmes, 1938, p 191)!" "Because Truth is Infinite, It must be continuously unfolding in the consciousness of man (Holmes, 1938, p 191)." All forms of worship continue to evolve, as do all those who worship. Through worship, the mind quiets, awareness grows and the directive of peace, love and harmony grows in that person's heart. True believers of all the major religions in the world, Christianity, Islam, Hinduism, Judaism, Buddhism, or any

nature based religion, believe in peace, love and harmony. We all have this in common.

"The [practitioner] will do all of [the] work [within], and will give his [or her] whole time and attention to correct knowing, but… will leave [the] patient free to use any method that will benefit [the patient] (Holmes, 1938, p 192)." We not only do not interfere with a person's choice of worship, but with a person's choice of treatment. Whatever a person believes will heal them, will heal them. "Without controversy, we work side by side with any doctor the patient may desire— we, in the field of [embodiment], the physician in his [or her] own field (Holmes, 1938, p 199)."

"Too much cannot be said against the belief that will power is creative. The will is directive but not creative. Will is the conscious, directive power of the intellect and as such has a very important place in the creative order but in no case is it to be used as though it could force things to happen. Any idea of using the will to influence people is a mistake. If we agree that we can influence others by will power, then we are also admitting that someone else with a greater power of will can influence us… Moreover this use of will power contradicts the main foundation upon which all true mental science is built, that we use a Creative Power which does not need to be urged or forced into action (Holmes, 1938, p 192)." This is the biggest distinction between a "by me" consciousness and an "as me" consciousness. It may be true that when we first learn to use our Creative Power, we must use our will to remind ourselves to disregard negative thinking and to begin the process of knowing the Truth of who we truly are. But, ultimately, our goal is to rest in that place of knowing, using our Creative Power from a perspective of understanding that we and the One Mind are one and any form we wish to manifest of course comes into physical form simply because we know it to be so.
"Concentration of thought is not an effort to compel, but the desire to permit, the stream of Creative Energy to take definite form (Holmes, 1938, p 193)."

"One of the most important things for us to remember is that we are always causing something to be created… (Holmes, 1938, p 194)." Consciously or unconsciously, our creative process is giving direction to the One Mind through the Law, creating our reality. The more we can understand and accept this fact, without blame, but with taking full responsibility, the more we can use our will to train ourselves to practice knowing Truth until we embody the Truth. We do not need will to know our heart is beating. Once the Truth is embodied, our will won't be needed to create. We will know that, of course, the form we visualize is already at hand, and it will be so.

"We are so One with the Whole that what is true of It is also true of us (Holmes, 1938, p 195)." We are not speaking of some power outside of us that we somehow communicate with and use. Just as there is not a God outside of us, there is not a Power outside of us. We must remember that we are this Power. We are the same Creative Force that created the heavens and the earth. To the exact level we can accept and embody this Truth about ourselves is to the exact level we create our lives consciously.

"Man has the ability to choose what he will do with his life, and is unified with a Law which automatically produces his choice (Holmes, 1938, p 196)." This is what makes being conscious of what we embody so important. The Law is producing our choice as a totality, not just the ones in which we are aware. "Man is an individual and does with himself what he wills (Holmes, 1938, p 196)." Free will gives us the ability to choose whatever we want; but free will may also lead to choices that create the discord we experience in our lives.

The discord we experience occurs when we are not in alignment with what Dr. Holmes calls, "Divine Givingness (Holmes,1938, p 43)." In the introduction chapter, part three, we discuss how there is a directive built into the fabric of the universe, evolving everything in it towards peace, love and harmony. This directive is a soft, gentle voice within us, which does not overpower our free will. Yet, like a consistent stream that can cut through a mountain over time, Its ever present nudge awaits our awareness, our enlightenment, to Its presence. Discord falls away when we let ourselves be influenced by this directive of Love that is in the very fabric of our being. We feel aligned with something greater than ourselves and connected to the rest of humanity and the planet.

This gentle directive is not asking us to give up our free will and lose what is unique and magnificent about our individuality. When we strike the balance between our free will and the quiet voice within us, we are not only healed, but creating at the level of the paintings created by Picasso. "The Divine Nature is re-enacted in [each of us]; [we are] conscious mind and spirit, and, as [we contemplate, we reflect our embodiment] into the Universal Subjectivity where it is received and acted upon (Holmes, 1938, p 196)."

"Healing, then, is accomplished by uncovering, neutralizing and erasing false images... , and letting the perfect idea reflect itself through subjective mind into the body (Holmes, 1938, p 197)." As we relax ever deeper into knowing the embodiment of our Divine Nature, we align ourselves with this quiet inner directive of Love. The more we express our Divine Nature and hold it as an image for those who have asked for treatment, healing must occur, because nothing else is the ultimate Truth of who we are. "Realizing that conscious thought operates through a Power which is Infinite, we see there can be no limit to the power to heal, other than the limit of our ability to conceive that Power as healing. We are limited, not by Principle, but by our own inability to see perfection (Holmes, 1938, p 197)."

"When a practitioner treats anyone, [the practitioner] does not just hope that [the] patient will get well, [and] does not ask that the patient may be healed, [the practitioner] does not simply desire that [the patient] may be healed (Holmes, 1938, p 198);" the practitioner embodies "an understanding that the patient is healed and is perfect (Holmes, 1938, p 198)." "Treatment does not necessarily treat every organ of the body specifically, but it does declare the body to be harmonious, and that every specific idea in it is harmonious (Holmes, 1938, p 198)." Because our Divine Nature is perfect health and well-being, it is as simple as embodying this image for ourselves and others. "The practitioner is not trying to send out a thought, hold a thought, or suggest a thought. The practitioner is trying to realize the state of perfection of the patient. We must be certain that we differentiate between suggestion (which is all right as far as it goes, but limited) and real metaphysical healing. In metaphysical healing, we are conscious that we are dealing with a Universal Principle or Law, which takes the impress of our [embodiment] and acts upon it. We are dealing with Something that cannot, and does not argue. We are directing It for definite purposes, telling It to do certain things, which It does. This is what occurs when we give a treatment (Holmes, 1938, p 199)."

"Regardless of its particular source, disease is an experience operating through people, which does not belong to them at all (Holmes, 1938, p 200)." We must never think of a disease as ours. The words, "my cold", "my ulcer", or whatever else we tend to claim ownership of that brings discord into our lives, are falsehoods. Because we have free will, the Law says yes to our ownership and it sticks that condition to our bodies like glue. It is up to us to change our relationship with whatever the form is we wish to let go of; release ownership and know that whatever the condition is, is not us or ours. "The first thing a practitioner does is to separate the belief from the believer. It is a personal, not a Cosmic problem. Evil is not a problem to God, it is only a problem to the individual (Holmes, 1938, p 201)." Evil does not exist in our Divine Nature. It only exists in our personalities to the extent we believe it exists. "If the practitioner is able to see only perfection, wholeness, he will see health manifested in his patient (Holmes, 1938, p 201)."

"You must know that the Power you are using is definite, scientific, dynamic, spiritual, absolute, complete, and that It will work. Let no fear come into your thought (Holmes, 1938, p 201)." "Begin to use this principle, no matter how slight you feel your knowledge, and the result will inspire you to perceive new ways and methods of approach, until you gradually grow into deeper assurance (Holmes, 1938, p 201)." As we practice, our embodiment deepens. Do not be disheartened by how slight you feel about how all this works. Let the process of practice inspire you. Let it carry you in ways you may never have experienced before. The Power of which we are speaking is within you. The more conscious you become of Its workings, the more you will bring into form the life of your dreams. Never doubt it. Keep practicing. There is only one conclusion possible. You are a powerful, creative, spiritual being and your life works.

"Diseases which are mental in their origin must arise from some inner state of consciousness. While most disease must first have a subjective cause, this subjective cause (nine times out of ten) is not conscious in the thought of the person who suffers from it, but is perhaps largely the result of certain combinations of thinking (Holmes, 1938, p 201)." This could include race consciousness, unconsciousness and the influence of those closest to you.

"The practitioner seeks to realize man as perfect, not needing to be healed of anything. This is nothing less than the realization of the Presence and the Power of God, or Spirit, as Humanity's Life, as the only life there is, as complete and perfect... right now (Holmes, 1938, p 202)." There is only one Truth in regards to disease, "The spiritual man needs no healing, health is an omnipresent reality, and when the obstructions that hinder healing are removed, it will be found that health was there all the time (Holmes, 1938, p 203)."

"Scientific mental healing is the result of clear thinking and logical reasoning, which presents itself to consciousness and is acted upon by Mind (Holmes, 1938, p 203)." Treatment is more than just words being spoken. It is using the Power of words to create a clear image in the mind of the Practitioner, which is also the One Mind, and the mind of the patient. Whatever words are used must be effective in creating this image of the Divine Nature of who we truly are. Whether they are spoken logically step- by-step to the conclusion of Perfection, or whether the conclusion of Perfection is known and embodied easily makes no difference in the One Mind. The only thing that makes a difference is that this conclusion of Perfection is reached, held and known. "Right thought, constantly poured into consciousness, will eventually purify it (Holmes, 1938, p 204)."

"A treatment is not complete without a great realization of Life and Love, of God and Perfection, of Truth and Wisdom, of Power and Reality. Sense the Divine Presence in and through the patient at all times (Holmes, 1938, p 205)." These characteristics of the Divine Nature must be embodied within ourselves first. The more we know our own Divine Nature, the easier it becomes to know it for others. "The practitioner is in the same Mind in which [the] patient lives (Holmes, 1938, p 205);" … thus, "The practitioner realizes a certain truth for [the] patient within [him or herself]. Therefore, [the practitioner] sets the Law in motion for [the] patient (Holmes, 1938, p 205)."

Just to be clear, "In practice, we make no attempt to send thoughts to our patients (Holmes, 1938, p 206)!" "To the degree that the practitioner brings his [or her] own consciousness to a true recognition of perfection— provided there is a subjective receptivity in the thought of the patient— that [patient] will be helped (Holmes, 1938, p 206)." All the work happens within the consciousness of the practitioner. Not by will, but by knowing. This is not about convincing the client of their perfection. It is all about knowing the client's perfection within the consciousness of the practitioner. But, of course, the practitioner must first know his or her own perfection, before the practitioner can know it for somebody else. That is why, when looking for a practitioner to work with, one that has already demonstrated what you desire to come into physical form is best.

"There is no peculiar sensation which accompanies a treatment, neither is it necessary that the practitioner should

71

feel anything, other than the truth of the words that he speaks (Holmes, 1938, p 207)." Though there are those who experience different forms of relaxation, light or other uplifting sensations, it is absolutely unnecessary to feel anything different for a treatment to be effective. The practitioner's ability to know the Truth is all that matters.

"The thing to remember is, that THERE IS JUST ONE SUBJECTIVE MIND IN THE UNIVERSE... If there is but One Subjective Mind in the Universe (and we have already learned the meaning and nature of Subjective Mind: It is deductive, receptive, plastic, neutral, impersonal and creative, It is the Stuff from which all things are made) you can impress upon It a certain image of thought, or a certain process of realization, and you will get a result, for It is the Actor (Holmes, 1938, p 208)." It is the realization, the embodiment of the form you want to see demonstrated, that is key here, for that form to come into being. "The very force which makes us sick can heal us, the force which makes us poor can enrich us, and the power which makes us miserable can make us happy. If this were not true, there would be a duality in the Universe and this is impossible (Holmes, 1938, p 209)."

"WILL-POWER HAS NOTHING WHATEVER TO DO WITH MENTAL HEALING (Holmes, 1938, p 210)!" Will power is part of our personality. "All thoughts of doubt concerning one's ability to heal, come from the belief that it is the personality and not the Law which does the healing (Holmes, 1938, p 210)."

"Remember that the thought of the parents influences the child (Holmes, 1938, p 210)." When working with children, especially young children, what they embody is very tied to what their parents embody. "Everything that opposes harmony and spontaneous unity, will prove disastrous to the child's health, sooner or later. After a certain age, children have to be re-educated, just as do adults, that their subjective mind may not reproduce false impressions (Holmes, 1938, p 211)." The more the parents embody their own Divine Nature, the more they can embody the same for their child. This does not mean the parents are involved, in any way, with the treatment of knowing perfection for the child. But, it is to the child's advantage to have parents who understand and use the One Mind in a conscious manner.

"A practitioner does not treat a sick man, he deals only with the idea, a spiritual man (Holmes, 1938, p 212);" because, a spiritual man is the ultimate Truth and the sickness is simply a physical form that can be changed by changing what we embody. "Healing is not creating a perfect idea or a perfect body; it is revealing an idea which is already perfect. Healing is not a process, it is a revelation, through the [embodiment] of the practitioner(Holmes, 1938, p 212)." We must remember to the best of our ability that "Disease is a fact but not a truth; it is an experience but not a spiritual reality (Holmes, 1938, p 213)." This is why we say there is nothing to heal, only Truth to be revealed. Healing is never the goal. Knowing the Truth of our well-being is. Whatever the condition, circumstance or experience, "we must try to see and sense that always, back of the appearance, PERFECTION IS (Holmes, 1938, p 214)."

Chapter 15: Physical Perfection, Concluded

"[I]f we are dealing with a Universal Principle, why should we set any limit to Its power? Since the Law of God is Infinite, from the spiritual viewpoint, there is no incurable disease, as opposed to a curable one (Holmes, 1938, p 215)." How can the same Power that created the Universe and everything in it not be able to cure anything that is in discord with Divine Nature? It has been mentioned time and time again throughout this book that we are not just a part of Divine Nature, we are Divine Nature. As such, what could be incurable? Miracles happen every day for those who embody themselves as perfect, whole and complete.

I was diagnosed with ulcerative colitis at the age of twelve. By twenty-eight, doctors told me I had so much scar tissue in my intestines, it was no longer a matter of *if* I got cancer, but *when*. Just before my fortieth birthday, doctors told me I had three days to live and there was nothing they could do to save me. At the writing of this book, I am fifty-eight years old and in the best health of my life. The last time doctors took a look at my intestines they said what they saw was impossible. The ulcerative colitis that had ravaged my intestines for over thirty years was not just in remission, but there was no sign of scarring of any kind, as if I had never had ulcerative colitis in the first place. I'd been seeing the same doctors from when I was sixteen and the best they could come up with was that they must have misdiagnosed me all those years and confused the photos of my intestines with those of another patient. But, what I know, is that knowing the Truth of who we are and embodying that Truth is the most powerful healing on earth. No discord or disease can stand in the face of Truth. By constantly treating for the wholeness, wellness and perfection of who I am, until the vision sunk into the cells of my being, of course, my health demonstrated. The outward appearance could be thought of as a healing. But, the Truth is my perfection always existed. Through realization of the Truth, the Truth became revealed.

Once I freely chose the wholeness I have always been, it showed up in my life.

We know that in treatment, focusing on individual organs is unnecessary for wholeness to show up in physical form— but, because we're not always aware of the totality of what we have embodied presently that might contradict wholeness, it may take some inner work for our wholeness to be revealed. Sometimes we think we are clear, when we have unconscious beliefs that are tipping the scale of demonstration away from us. When we treat regularly, but have not yet manifested in physical form what we are treating for, sometimes what happens first is those unconscious beliefs surface for us to shed like a snake sheds its skin, unveiling the deeper Truth. Sometimes it takes a process of digging deep within ourselves, pulling out the weeds so our true self may flower. "The sincere practitioner will be sure his own thought is clear, that his own faith is equal to the demands made upon it. Above all else he must be careful not to be caught in the negative stream of consciousness (Holmes, 1938, p 217)." The practitioner cannot do the work from a consciousness of believing the condition has, in any way, shape or form, power, or is a "problem." All form takes shape from the level of consciousness, out of the One Mind. All form takes shape because we make it so.

"In beginning a series of treatments for any person, we start with the idea of Perfect God, Perfect [Person], and Perfect Being (Holmes, 1938, p 218)." "We must relight the torch of our imagination by "fire caught from heaven." We must remain faithful to this vision for a realization of the Presence of God is the secret power of our work (Holmes, 1938, p 218)." "Infinite Love harmonizes [our] entire being. The healing currents of Life flow through [us], taking away every negative thought and manifestation, and adjusting [our] whole physical being to the idea of Divine Harmony (Holmes, 1938, p 219)." Once we have embodied Divine Harmony, all things are not only possible, but the miraculous is inevitable.

But, until such time that we have completely embodied Divine Harmony, it is good to remember, "Since our spiritual understanding is not sufficient to enable us to mentally set bones, we call in a surgeon; since we cannot walk on the water, we take a boat. We can go only as far as our spiritual [embodiment] takes us. Principle is Infinite, but we shall demonstrate Its power only at the level of our [embodiment] of It (Holmes, 1938, p 219)." "If we had the [embodiment] which Jesus had, we would be able to walk on the water (Holmes, 1938, p 219)." As our understanding and embodiment grows, so does our ability to miraculously create. It's not one extreme or the other. It's a matter of all the degrees of embodiment in-between.

Nor does this embodiment of Divine Harmony need be about everything to take form in a particular area of our lives. One may have a deep embodiment around abundance and, so easily create riches. Yet, have very little embodiment around health, so as to experience disease. Another may embody a beautiful vision of being a source of nurturing for others, yet, may not embody very much around self-nurturance. So it is that we can know by what is currently demonstrating in physical form, what areas of our lives we've embodied our vision we want to create and what areas still need our attention.

"[O]ne treatment would heal if there were no subjective doubts. Repeated treatments induce, within consciousness, a definite concept of an already established truth, even though the fact may not as yet have become objectified. This is why mental healing is scientific. There is no room for doubt in a treatment (Holmes, 1938, p 220)." We repeat treatment until there is no doubt and the form to be realized is entirely embodied. How do we know when we've completely embodied the form we want realized? When what we are treating for shows up in physical form.

"Principle is the Power that made everything. It is Absolute, It will not and cannot be denied... Do not think of disease as an entity, but as an impersonal thought-force. In

77

healing, you are separating the false from the true. The work is definite and dynamic, and is consciously done, always with a clear purpose in mind (Holmes, 1938, p 221)." This is why we say there is nothing to heal, only Truth to be revealed. Disease is an experience, not a reality; not an ultimate Truth. The more we affirm the experience of disease, the more we solidify the form in the physical. We do not deny the experience of the disease, for that would be lying to ourselves. We simply do not claim the condition as ours, nor as an entity which has any power over us. This is a really important distinction. It is not just a matter of semantics. We must remember that words have power and that our entire universe, especially our bodies respond to how we say and hold things. By acknowledging the experience as simply an experience, rather than something more than that, we allow our consciousness to transform, first our perception and then the physical form itself. "When you give a treatment, you are definitely setting a Universal Law in motion, which must not only accept what you say but the way in which you say it. If your treatment is given with a sense of struggle, it will manifest in that way. If it is given with a sense of peace, then it will manifest in a peaceful manner (Holmes, 1938, p 221)." Also, "You cannot heal anyone of his trouble, if it is the result of some mental attitude which he will not surrender (Holmes, 1938, p 222)."

What follows is a list of conditions and the best thinking to embody the health in physical form one might desire. Again, we do not need to treat about the particular condition. It is our job in Science of Mind to always know the perfection which must be in every cell that may appear and have the experience of imperfection. Still, to help us weed out the imperfections and know the Truth, it may be helpful to understand what the possible underlying beliefs and embodiments that might be associated with a particular condition. I have added very little commentary to Dr. Holmes' words in the rest of this chapter. I have done my best to list the gems as I perceive them.

How Habits Are Acquired and Treated

"At the root of all habit is one basic thing: the desire to express life... Some express themselves constructively and some destructively. Suppose a man who has the liquor habit comes to you to be healed. You would not treat that habit. You would not pray for the man to be healed. You would know that you are dealing with a man who has the desire to express life and who, for the moment, thinks he must express it in terms of intoxication... This thing which calls itself the liquor habit has no power over him and cannot operate through him (Holmes, 1938, p 223)." What we know for this man, or anyone coming to us with a habit they would like to release, is that they are "free and harmoniously expressing life and happiness (Holmes, 1938, p 223)."

Treating Pain

"Use the thought of peace with the realization of a Perfect Presence (Holmes, 1938, p 223)." It is our instinct to try our best to run from pain, but we cannot escape our bodies. Embody peace and harmony, knowing for ourselves or whomever we are treating for, that pain is no different than any other condition or experience and the deeper we can embody wellbeing, the less pain we will feel. "Know this until there comes to your consciousness a deep, calm sense of peace and ease, and until every thought of pain is eliminated (Holmes, 1938, p 224)."

Repeating Treatments

"Always come to a complete conclusion when giving a treatment. Always feel that it is done, complete and perfect, and give thanks for the answer, as if it were already objectified. In the interval between treatments, do not carry the thought of the patient around with you. To do so is to doubt, and this mental attitude must be completely overcome... The treatment should be repeated daily until a healing takes place. If it takes five minutes, five hours, five days, or five years, the treatment must be kept up until a healing is accomplished. This is the only method we know. It is not enough to say that everything is all right. This is true in Principle, but in fact and in human experience, it is only as true as we make it. Treat until you get results. A healing takes place when the patient is no longer sick, and until such time, mental work should be done (Holmes, 1938, p 224)."

Headache

"A treatment for peace, alone, often brings quick results when one is suffering from headache (Holmes, 1938, p 225)." Dr. Holmes speaks of the "mental knot, that needs to be untied... (Holmes, 1938, p 225)." This is always the case with any ailment. Somehow we have tied our beliefs or what we embody to something that is causing our body's distress. When we can fully relax and trust in the perfection of our lives and the knowing that our lives work, suffering disappears.

Why People Become Fatigued

"Let a person say to himself, "I am overworked," and at once there will come up through his consciousness a belief in weariness. People who are constantly complaining of being tired are hypnotized into this belief through the law of race suggestion (Holmes, 1938, p 226)." "We can free ourselves from a feeling of approaching fatigue, by knowing that we have within us— always immediately available— an Infinite Strength... This power within you is the same that holds the planets in space. The power back of your word is perfect law and is fulfilled and returned to you as your perfect strength (Holmes, 1938, p 227)."

Treating Insanity

"In treating one whose mind appears to be deranged, realize that there is but One Mind, which Mind is God, and is Perfect. This is the only Mind there is. It is the Mind of your patient; It is your own Mind. This Mind being a Complete, Perfect, and Indivisible Whole, cannot labor under a delusion, cannot for one moment lose Its Self-Consciousness. After you have realized this Truth about Life, know that it is also true about the one whom you are treating (Holmes, 1938, p 227)."

Treating Lung Trouble

"Back of all such trouble is a consuming passion, an unexpressed emotion, a strong desire. The practitioner realizes there is a perfect body, perfect being, perfect God, perfect man, perfect expression, perfect bronchial tubes, perfect trachea, perfect lungs (Holmes, 1938, p 228)!" By knowing this Truth, "the patient will be relieved, though the practitioner never thinks of [the] patient, other than that the word of Truth is being spoken for [the patient]. [The practitioner] never wonders whether [the treatment] is taking effect, because [the practitioner] speaks into Intelligence and lets It act (Holmes, 1938, p 229)." We must practice day in and day out until we know with absolute certainty "[that the] Substance out of which our bodies are] created is Spiritual, and is maintained by the all-powerful Essence of Spirit (Holmes, 1938, p 229)."

Vision

"The mind within does the real seeing, the real interpreting of what the eyes look upon. The eyes can truly be called "the windows of the soul… There is no obstruction to vision, no near vision and no far vision; there is no false vision, no weak vision nor blurred vision. There is One Perfect Seeing, which is now seeing through you [and as you] ... which is now seeing through me [and as me]… Always one should be conscious of the idea of Wholeness of Life, perfect function at every point (Holmes, 1938, p 230)."

Constipation

"Constipation is often due to a belief in limitation or burden, and is mentally helped by knowing that there is no restriction, no inaction, no limited action, no bondage, no fear, no congestion. Realize that all action is normal, harmonious and perfect (Holmes, 1938, p 231)." "Any kind of fear thought retards the free action of the life forces, thus greatly interfering with the functions of the body. In such cases a treatment for complete relaxation should be given. It is well to know: "Infinite Intelligence ... controls and directs all of the organs of my body, so that they function perfectly according to their nature. I am an open channel for good to flow in and through me, freely, generously, cheerfully... Thoughts of peace and good will, a recognition of the unity of all men, will produce harmony, and bring about perfect elimination in the body. It is [also] necessary that we release all thoughts— as well as things— that clutter up our lives (Holmes, 1938, p 232)."

"A thought of Love is always healing, and particularly so in the case of constipation. If the practitioner has a full realization that Love fulfills all the laws of life— his life and the patient's life— that there are no restrictions, no burdens, no inhibitions in Love, which is the very life within, healing will follow. If one would take time, once a day at least, to let go of... doubt, distrust, worry, condemnation and fear, and lay hold of Life in Its expressions of beauty, truth and wholeness, his mental congestion would be healed (Holmes, 1938, p 233)."

Skin

"The skin represents a temporary, but perfect, outward cloak, forever responsive to that deep, inner calm, that place where Life is poised in Itself (Holmes, 1938, p 234)."

Arms and Hands

"The arms and hands represent man's ability to grasp ideas. To uphold... convictions of the truth (Holmes, 1938, p 234)."

Feet and Legs

"The feet and legs represent man's ability to walk uprightly. To be guided into all truth. To be led by the ever-present Mind (Holmes, 1938, p 234)."

False Growths (Tumors, Cancer, Gallstones)

"Destructive emotions, desires or ideas, unless neutralized, will grow into some bodily condition, and may produce disease... If the thought of false growths can be erased, the manifestation can be healed (Holmes, 1938, p 234)." All of these are demonstrations that spring from our free will to believe and embody anything, even if it is not for our highest good. Even if we are unconscious of what it is we are embodying.

It is amazing how many people have declared having cancer and living through it as the greatest blessing of their lives. This could only be true because they have awakened to the higher Truth of who they truly are, and by expressing that Truth, the cancer not only disappeared, but their lives are transformed. "Whether it be cancer, fibroid tumor, a wen, a cyst, or gallstones, the practitioner must know that the Spirit indwelling [the] patient is perfectly and completely manifested, and that every shadow of erroneous conclusion is wiped out (Holmes, 1938, p 236)." Of course, if "every shadow of erroneous conclusion is wiped out," the patient will live in an enlightened state like never before in their lives.

Removing the Complex

"Suppose someone is constantly saying: "Everything is all wrong in the world. People are wrong, things are wrong, conditions are wrong. All is sickness and unhappiness. Nothing seems worthwhile." You as a practitioner must not be disturbed by this complaint. It is your business to remove this complex, for these inner emotions create outer conditions, in and through the body, and are responsible for a great deal of sickness in the world. Treatment straightens out consciousness by clear thinking. When the inner consciousness agrees with the Truth, then— and not until then— a demonstration takes place (Holmes, 1938, p 236)." "We [, as practitioners,] recognize that everything is in Mind and that nothing moves but Mind. That Intelligence is back of everything, acting through a thought force which is concrete, definite and real (Holmes, 1938, p 237)." When we understand that our Divinity is expressing Itself through our humanity, we open to the good that is our birthright and perceive the world accordingly.

Heart Trouble

"The heart is the center of Divine Love and perfect circulation. Its action is harmonious, vital, adequate and complete. There is no false action and no wrong action. The pulsations of life are steady, unceasing and perfect. "Let not your heart be troubled." Love is at the center of [our] being, and the calm, continuous, pulsations of life are governed by Love (Holmes, 1938, p 238)."

"Almost every case of heart trouble can be traced to thoughts of strain and inharmony; sometimes to disappointment or disagreement with a loved one; or to a feeling of loss from financial reverses… The heart is known as the center of love, which is the healing balm for every inharmonious thought. As we recognize our Oneness with Infinite Intelligence, we are set free from uncertainty and pain. As long as we realize that our heart is a living center, through which the Love of God flows to bless eternally, not only our own lives but the lives of all whom we contact— as long as we realize this, our heart cannot be troubled (Holmes, 1938, p 239)."

Poison of Any Kind

"The treatment is similar in all cases of poison. The healing must come through a recognition that the body is pure Spirit substance (Holmes, 1938, p 240)."

Paralysis

"Use the thought that Life cannot become paralyzed or inactive... As in constipation, there is a thought of restriction back of the manifestation of paralysis; often there is a very emotional nature to deal with, and often, though not always, a lot of stubbornness and resistance to heal (Holmes, 1938, p 240)."

"[The patient] must be shown that in Mind there is perfect freedom, and that in this freedom nothing can [be bound], either mentally or physically, that nothing which [was] ever [done] or thought or that anyone else did or thought, can bind [the patient], that the very Life of God is... freedom, that this Infinite Life and Action compels [the patient] to act out the truth about [him or herself] on the objective plane... When Jesus healed the paralyzed man, He first made him whole in consciousness, then told him to take up his bed and walk... The practitioner should know, without shadow of doubt, that the very power by which the paralytic took up his bed and walked— the power by which Jesus raised His body— is exactly the same power by which paralyzed legs and arms are vitalized and made whole today (Holmes, 1938, p 241)."

Asthma and Hay Fever

"We should know that the claim of hay fever has no power over us, that we are inspired and directed by Infinite Mind, and that perfect discrimination and judgment are established in us (Holmes, 1938, p 242)." "The pollen which you have thought irritated you is made from the very same Substance from which you are made. You are sending out only thoughts of peace, love and joy, and no irritating thought or thing can come back to annoy or obstruct the perfect functioning of every organ of your body. The passages of your mind are open only to the inflow and the outflow of good... Let your thought dwell, not on breath nor lack of breath, but on that which breathes (Holmes, 1938, p 243)."

Nerve Troubles

"Our thought is creative, not because we will it so, but BECAUSE IT ALREADY IS SO... Consequently we see that certain thoughts would depress while others would exalt... The general treatment for nerve disorders should incorporate thoughts of peace, poise and power. There is no strain or struggle in the Universe. All the actions of Life are harmonious, steady, sure and quiet (Holmes, 1938, p 244)." "An understanding of the truth that good alone is real and true, gives us the faith essential to an establishment of a firm, unwavering mind, which is necessary if one is to have firm, steady, sensitive, quickly-responding nerves (Holmes, 1938, p 245)."

"We must heal ourselves from worry. This tension is relaxed as we gain confidence in good, in truth and in beauty. Faith must overcome fear, and strong statements of faith should be used to erase the thoughts of doubt and worry that have assailed us. "I have faith. I am faith. I abide in faith. All doubt and fear have left me. I understand why it is that I can remain in faith. I have complete confidence. I do not waver nor falter in my faith, for I know that God, the Living Spirit, is the only Presence there is or ever can be (Holmes, 1938, p 245)."

"We live in a sea of Perfect Life and we should take time to understand and sense this in our imagination... We should hold out the cup of acceptance until it is filled and overflowing with the manifestations of our desires... We are poised in a sense of peace, which comes from our complete faith in God as the light, power and inspiration of our life (Holmes, 1938, p 246)."

Blood Troubles and Skin Diseases (High Blood Pressure, Hardening of the Arteries, Eczema, Boils)

"The blood stream represents the circulation of pure thought, direct from a Divine Source. The metabolism represents the intelligence within [each of us] which knows

86

what to use, and what to cast out. This blood stream represents the spiritual flow of life, pure and perfect... This stream of life is renewed daily. It is not material, but spiritual. The blood stream is continuously renewed as it converts the idea of Spiritual Substance into material benefits. Love, harmony and peace reign supreme. The arteries convey this blood stream, and neither harden nor soften. They are always flexible, always perfect. There is no tension nor super-tension, but always a calm flow of life forever invigorating, forever renewing, forever revitalizing, carrying to every part of the body and distributing in every part of the body, pure spiritual substance, instantly and permanently perfect (Holmes, 1938, p 247)."

"A deep-seated resentment against persons or conditions will surely manifest itself in some disagreeable physical reaction. The first step toward healing is one of honest self-analysis (Holmes, 1938, p 248)." "Treat to know that Love is stronger than any other force in the Universe, and that steadily and rhythmically the Life of God is pulsing through your body (Holmes, 1938, p 249)." "[As a practitioner,] you sense this person as being Divine, the Spirit indwells him... Nothing can impoverish [your patient's] flow; nothing can increase or diminish that pressure (Holmes, 1938, p 250)." Know that you, or your patient, are "harmonious, peaceful, free and unafraid (Holmes, 1938, p 250)."

Fevers

"In mind healing the underlying thought in the treatment for fever, is Peace. Any thought which tends to inspire, to comfort and to give peace to the mind is good (Holmes, 1938, p 250)." "A general treatment like the following will be found effective in allaying fever: "At all times, I am aware of my immediate Oneness with God; and the glory of my thought makes me immune to negative experiences, even to negative suggestions. I desert fear and turn resolutely and joyously to faith, and swiftly into my experience comes the desired good. I give thanks that I am Divine and that I know my Divinity. A sacred refuge is this inner place where my thought contacts

87

and consciously becomes one with the Indwelling Almighty (Holmes, 1938, p 251)"."

Obstetrics

"In a treatment for child-birth, we realize that the great Law of Creation is operative. We know that no idea of God ever comes too soon or too late, but always at the correct time. We know that right action prevails... Realize that Perfection is at work, forming and projecting into the objective world that upon which Its action has been centered; that there can be no obstruction to right action on any plane of expression (Holmes, 1938, p 251)."

Colds, Influenza and Grippe

"Those who calmly announce that they are "very susceptible to changes in the weather," have accepted whole-heartedly the mental impression that the weather is a determining factor in whether or not they experience "colds..." In colds, congestion, influenza and grippe, the thought to heal is confusion. There should be a consciousness of poise, a recognition of peace; when this comes into the individual's experience, he will have fewer colds (Holmes, 1938, p 252)."

Obesity

"A normally-minded person will eat normally. If one is a glutton, it is because [this person]... is filled with unexpressed longings, which [the person] is trying to sublimate... [T]here is a difference between feeding your hunger and your appetite... [D]eclare that you are an offspring of God, that you are Spirit, that both your appetite and the assimilation of your foods are functioning in divine order, and that your body is manifesting symmetry and perfection (Holmes, 1938, p 253)."

Treating Kidney, Bladder and Liver Disturbances

"Mental agencies which contribute to the production of all kinds of kidney trouble are worry, anxiety, fear, and criticism... The conscious knowledge that in Divine Mind we are known only as perfection so uplifts the thought that every mental and emotional reaction to circumstances and conditions is improved (Holmes, 1938, p 253)." Declare, "My kidneys perform their natural function and are adjusted to their natural and spiritual perfection and operation. They are perfect because they are spiritual ideas and all that God conceived is now perfect... My blood stream is pure, perfect and spiritual. I sense this, know it and understand it (Holmes, 1938, p 254)."

"In treating bladder trouble it is well to calm the thought. To remove any sense of inner irritation or agitation will always be of great value in removing this particular trouble... Purity and strength, with perfect elimination, free from any sense of condemnation, is a good central thought to work on (Holmes, 1938, p 254)."

"Thoughts of greed, selfishness and jealousy cause congestion in various functions of the body, especially the kidneys... with thoughts of anger, hatred and resentment, we are pouring into our body poisons in the making (Holmes, 1938, p 255)."

"Just as the liver can convert certain substances into building material for the body, so the mind— filled with the knowledge that there is but One Divine, Powerful, Vital Essence— can change inharmonious thoughts into ideas that heal, cleanse and uplift (Holmes, 1938, p 255)."

Treating Stomach and Bowel Troubles

"No organ in the body is more quickly upset by a disturbed mental condition than is the stomach. Frequently people, not even familiar with the manner in which thought controls the body, are heard to remark that a certain experience has "upset my stomach..." The very best mental remedy for stomach trouble is love and joy... Declare, "The very life of God vitalizes my every organ and tissue. I now have perfect and complete faith in God as my ever-present Good (Holmes, 1938, p 256)"."

Treating Insomnia

"Insomnia is the result of a disturbed mental condition, either conscious or subconscious... Perfect trust in God within is the secret of relaxation, rest and renewal (Holmes, 1938, p 257)." Declare, "The Spirit within me is in perfect rest. The center of my being is quiet and poised. I let my inner spirit fill my whole being with peace and stillness. With this word, I now relax in body and mind. I let the Divine Tranquillity fill me... My mind is quiet, calm, and deeply still. All tension is released and the great inner peace flows out through every nerve. My body rests in the still silence of the Spirit. I bless my body and my mind, for they are good and worthy of my love. The great blessing of the Spirit pours through me now and protects me in all my ways. My good is around and with me so that I am secure and safe. The loving presence of Spirit is with me now and forever, so that I am divinely protected (Holmes, 1938, p 257)."

Deafness

"The ear is the physical representation of a receptive capacity of mind... We can so train our ears to listen to the Divine Harmony within, that we shall reproduce Its melody, rhythm and beauty in all our ways... Hearing is a divine idea in Mind, and all divine ideas are perfect. Ideas have a service to render to the Spirit of man, and as long as man expects and accepts whole-heartedly that service, and co-operates consciously and subjectively with it, there is nothing to oppose the functioning of the physical instruments through which ideas operate (Holmes, 1938, p 258)." Declare, "My ears are open to the Divine Harmony. The inner ear and the outer ear are both open and receptive to the vibration of perfect harmony (Holmes, 1938, p 258)"."

Weather Conditions

"All weather is a manifestation of Spirit, a flowering of the Divine in sunshine, in shade, in rain and in clouds. Say:… Every atom of my body responds to this understanding that changes in weather conditions are but variations of the One Life, but different manifestations of the One God appearing to me in many forms (Holmes, 1938, p 258)."

Thoughts about Food

"Food must be a spiritual idea. It must be an idea of substance and supply. Since the food which we take into the system is fundamentally one with the body which receives it, there is no reason in Spirit why our food should harm us… Whatever our individual physical system needs to make it harmonious, Intelligence will guide us to. But we cannot expect to have our food agree with us if we are constantly condemning it (Holmes, 1938, p 259)."

Rheumatism

"There is no bondage in the Spirit and we should endeavor to realize that the Spirit frees us from every type of bondage… It is well to remind ourselves that the system is spiritual and divinely ordained (Holmes, 1938, p 260)." I wish to note here that Dr. Holmes speaks of being "washed clean by the Spirit [as having] real meaning to us and the practitioner should believe that there is such a baptism of Spirit as this (Holmes, 1938, p 260)." Though baptism does not have any real meaning for me, I mention this for those who might relate to this particular image. For me, it always comes back to unveiling the Truth of who we are as perfect, complete and divine. Unveiling the Truth and washing away the untruth, were close enough images to mention both. Both are correct. It is merely a matter of what works for you.

Bondage and freedom are but the two possibilities of our use of the Law. Let us affirm freedom, not bondage (Holmes, 1938, p 260)." Declare, "I have perfect and complete circulation of love, truth and beauty through my entire system... My body is the body of God, the Living Spirit Almighty (Holmes, 1938, p 261)"."

Healing Intemperance

"The Spirit within... does not long for anything. It is free, safe, and satisfied... There is no pleasure in intemperance, nor can it offer any suggestion of happiness... see this habit for exactly what it is, an illusion, which seeks to force [us] to believe that there is some power outside [ourselves] which can give... either pleasure or pain (Holmes, 1938, p 261)." "[The practitioner] must have a calm, unfaltering trust in... [revealing what's real], and in so doing, [freeing the physical] from... false belief (Holmes, 1938, p 262)."

Supply

"God is Spirit. Spirit is Substance and Substance is supply. This is the keynote to a realization of the more abundant life, to the demonstration of success in financial matters (Holmes, 1938, p 262)." Declare, "I am led, guided and inspired by the Living Spirit of Love and of right action. I am compelled to move in the right direction and to always know what to do, where, and how to do it. "I am surrounded by right action. I am filled with the consciousness of right action. Right action is success in all that I undertake to do. I am successful in all my undertakings, and I am compensated for all my efforts. I am surrounded by Substance, which is always taking the form of supply and always manifesting Itself to me in the form of whatever my need may be at the time... All good is now mine and is now manifest in my experience... There is that in me which all people recognize as worth while and desirable, and everyone whom I meet loves this self of mine and recognizes its worth... I have abundance, because I am abundance (Holmes, 1938, p 263)."

A Treatment for Peace of Mind

"We cannot be in peace until we know that the Spirit is the only cause, medium and effect in our lives. There is no past, present and future to It. Evil has no history and has never entered in to the being or the experience of Reality (Holmes, 1938, p 264)." Declare, "I am the Principle of Peace within me. I am the manifestation of Love within me. My mind is poised in peace and beauty. All sense of fear or doubt is gone. I rest in calm trust and rely on the Law of Spirit to bring good into my experience... I contend with none, argue with none, and am filled with wonderful peace and light. There is no uncertainty about my future and no fear as a result of my past. I live in an eternal Now which is filled with good alone. Goodness and beauty follow me. Peace and joy accompany me. Happiness and wholeness fill my entire being with the realization of love and perfection... I am the spirit of confidence. I am poised in love and reason. I am the perfect law of truth and the complete presence of beauty.... I am Christ, the Son of the Living God within me (Holmes, 1938, p 264)."

Chapter 16: The Principles of Successful Living

"Science of Mind is not a "get-rich-quick" scheme, neither does it promise something for nothing. It does, however, promise the one who will comply with its teachings that he shall be able to bring greater possibilities and happier conditions into his experience (Holmes, 1938, p 266)." Like many of the deepest teachings, it's simple but not easy.

Those who profess to think they understand our teachings while calling us positive thinkers do not realize the breadth and depth it takes to truly embody something that has not yet been embodied. Nor to transform something that has been embodied into something else. As we have stated, our conscious minds are the tip of the iceberg. Our lives are being created out of the deepest parts of ourselves. This is what we mean by embodiment. Take all the conscious thoughts, all the unconscious thoughts, all the beliefs, conscious and unconscious, mix them together like flavoring a soup and that's what our lives taste like. "[I]f we comply with the Law, the Law complies with us. No man can demonstrate peace and cling to unhappiness. He can demonstrate resignation, and call it peace, but it will not be peace. No man can jump into the water and remain dry. This is contrary to law and to reason. NO PERSON WHOSE ENTIRE TIME IS SPENT IN THE CONTEMPLATION OF LIMITATION CAN DEMONSTRATE FREEDOM FROM SUCH LIMITATION! The Law Itself must be willing to give, because in so giving Life is Self-Expressed (Holmes, 1938, p 267)." We provide the flavoring; the Law gives us the soup, our lives, to experience.

The simple part is we can see what we embody, by what we are creating. We can see the whole soup, mixed together by the experience of our lives. And, just like any good cook, we can change the flavor of the soup of our life by adding different seasoning. This is the not so easy part.

The more our thoughts align with the Universal Good, the more our lives will taste good. Any thought we habitually think will ultimately become a belief and beyond that, be embodied. To have these habitual thoughts be aligned with Universal Good comes at a price: we must be willing to let go of those thoughts that are in discord with our good, some of which we have carried from a very early age. "The Law through which man operates is Infinite, but man appears to be finite; that is, he has not yet evolved to a complete understanding of himself... As his understanding unfolds, his possibilities of attainment will increase (Holmes, 1938, p 267)."

"MAN MUST BECOME MORE IF HE WISHES TO DRAW A GREATER GOOD INTO HIS LIFE (Holmes, 1938, p 267)." This is the true heart of our teaching. We may start with positive thinking, but to draw a greater good into our lives, we must become that greater good. We must be more. "We provide the mold for the Creative Law, and unless the mold we provide is increased, Substance cannot increase in our experience; ... EVERY MAN MUST PAY THE PRICE FOR THAT WHICH HE RECEIVES AND THAT PRICE IS PAID IN MENTAL AND SPIRITUAL COIN (Holmes, 1938, p 268)." Do the work, receive the benefit.

"But this teaching should not be confused with the idea that we can show people how to get what they want, regardless (Holmes, 1938, p 268)." Because each of us is unique in how we express the Divine, what we manifest must be in alignment with our higher, greater, unique selves. This teaching is about manifesting that which you have come here to be. One of the amazing results that come from embodying Science of Mind Principles is that, no matter what we thought we wanted, we can discover deeper dreams that, when realized, bring us a greater satisfaction and fulfillment than we ever thought possible. Within the framework of who we have come here to be, that is the place where anything is possible.

"Anything that will enable us to express greater life, greater happiness, greater power— so long as it does not harm anyone— must be the Will of God for us. As much life as [we] can conceive will become a part of [our] experience (Holmes, 1938, p 269)." When you are looking at what you want, ask your higher self, "Does the thing I wish to do express more life, more happiness, more peace to myself... (Holmes, 1938, p 270)?" If the answer is "yes", then it is in alignment with who you have come here to be, which is the key to creating a fulfilling, love-filled life. "With this in mind, and believing that there is an Infinite Law of the Spirit, or Law of Life, which tends to multiply our gifts, because in so doing It multiplies Its own experience, Its own pleasure, Its own fruition; we may assume that spiritual man is already a success, is already supplied with everything that he needs. The potential of all things exists in the Universal Wholeness (Holmes, 1938, p 270)."

"We can demonstrate at the level of our ability to know. Beyond this, we cannot go. But we will constantly expand and increase in knowledge and understanding, thereby continuously growing in our ability to make use of the Law. In time, we shall be made free through It (Holmes, 1938, p 271)." This is what makes our teaching so rich and yet, not so easy. Whatever we wish to create, we must first embody. To embody anything that is not already in us takes practice, care, understanding and the desire to know ourselves.

"The way to work is to begin right where we are and, through constantly applying ourselves to the Truth, we gradually increase in wisdom and understanding, for in this way alone will good results be obtained (Holmes, 1938, p 271)." The best way to begin is, "The student should take time every day to see his life as he wishes it to be, to make a mental picture of his ideal. He should pass this picture over to the Law and go about his business, with a calm assurance that on the inner side of life something is taking place (Holmes, 1938, p 271)." It is this "calm assurance" that we wish to embody. It is a knowing that our lives manifest what we picture into existence, because it already lives in the Mind of God, even before we can see it.

97

"If, in the making of a demonstration, it becomes necessary to change our mode of living, then the Law will point the way and we will follow (Holmes, 1938, p 272)." True embodiment is more than holding a picture in our minds. It is living the life we dream to live. Sometimes that includes big or small changes in lifestyle, eating habits, with whom we socialize or any other habits that interfere with our being in alignment with who we have come here to be.

"People often say: "I don't know what to do; I don't know how to make a choice." We must realize that there is an Intelligence within us that does know. This "guidance" is just as true in India, where people are Buddhists, as it is in America where people are Christians. It was just as true ten thousand years ago, before the advent of Christianity, as it will be ten thousand years hence (Holmes, 1938, p 272)." The Spiritual Principle we are working with has existed since the beginning of time. Infinite Mind is exactly that, infinite. If we can quiet our not knowing long enough to listen, the part of us that knows will be heard. "There is a Divine Intelligence that knows the right answer,… and when we conceive new ideas, it is an act of the Divine projecting Itself into Creation (Holmes, 1938, p 273)."

"Treatment is not mental coercion; it is not will power; it is not concentration. We shall never arrive at a correct method of spiritual treatment merely by learning how to concentrate for any length of time on a particular object (Holmes, 1938, p 274)." Again, it is the "calm assurance" that, of course, what we have treated for is already done, because it is in the One Mind and must be so. "Treatment is not something one does to another, not something one does to an environment, nor to a situation. It is always the thing one does to himself (Holmes, 1938, p 274)." Because, within ourselves is the One Mind, which is everything, so that what we know within ourselves touches everything without.

"We already live in a Perfect Universe but It needs to be mentally seen and spiritually experienced before It can become a part of our everyday life (Holmes, 1938, p 274)." Shifting our perception shifts everything. Embodying that new perception is the difference between a momentary "ah ha" and a demonstration that changes your life forever. When we "train our thought to recognize the Spirit in everything we do, say or think (Holmes, 1938, p 276)," we can ultimately embody "[a] constant realization of the presence of Spirit [that] will provide a sense of Divine Companionship that no other attitude could produce (Holmes, 1938, p 276)." "When Jesus healed people and told them to get up and walk, He did not pray that they might be able to get up and walk. He exercised an authority which seemed to be the result of His communion with the Spirit, and undoubtedly it was. Practice is a definite statement in mind, a positive affirmation. It is an active, conscious, aggressive mental movement and in such degree as it embodies an idea— and there is no longer anything in our minds which denies the idea— it will take form (Holmes, 1938, p 277)."

"What we need to know is the Truth. This does not mean that we need not be active; of course we shall be active, but we need not compel things to happen (Holmes, 1938, p 277)." There is a huge difference between taking action out of a perception of willing things to happen, which is a "by me" level of consciousness, and the action we take coming forth out of the embodiment of who we have come here to be, which is an "as me" level of consciousness.

When we take action from the center of our being, with the "calm assurance" of knowing ourselves to be this Infinite Intelligence that is all there is, there is no stress, worry, panic or even urgency. We act from a perspective of time being on our side and our lives working magnificently. "Principle is Absolute, and in so far as any individual can actually induce, within consciousness, upon Principle, a definite, concrete acceptance of [the] desire ... it will manifest, even though every thought on earth had to change to compel it! If it were a bit of information that was needed for the demonstration that only one person on earth knew— and that person was in the center of Africa— the information would be produced (Holmes, 1938, p 277)!"

Chapter 17: Mental Equivalents

"If we know that the Power with which we are dealing is Principle and not personality; if we know and believe that Mind is the only Actor, Cause, Effect, Substance, Intelligence, Truth and Power that there is; if we have a real embodiment; then we can demonstrate. If we lack, if we are poor, if we are without friends, if we are without opportunity, we should be sure to erase from our consciousness any sense of lack. We erase thought from consciousness by pouring in an opposite thought. This thought meets the other and neutralizes its effect. It rubs it out just as we rub a chalk mark off a board. We must maintain a consistent, positive, aggressive mental attitude in the Truth. We walk by falling forward; water falls by its own weight; the planets are eternally falling through space; everything sustains itself in nature. The only reason man is limited is that he has not allowed the Divine within him to more completely express. Man's Divine Individuality compels Infinity to appear in his experience as duality because he has believed in duality (Holmes, 1938, p 279)."   If we have lack, in any area of our lives, no matter what we think we believe, the truth of what we embody is shown by what actually shows up in physical form. This is not a "fake it till you make it" teaching.   It is an immersing in the waters of Truth time and time and time again until it cleanses away any false embodiment about the nature of who we truly are. And, then continuing to bathe in the Truth as it grows into the "calm assurance" that is our birthright.

"Jesus revealed the nature of the Divine Being by his personal embodiment of the Divine Nature. He said, "As ye believe, it shall be done unto you." The whole teaching of Jesus was based on the theory that we are surrounded by an intelligent Law, which does unto each as he believes. He implied the necessity of faith, conviction, and acceptance. That is, it must be measured out to us according to our own measuring. We must not only believe, we must know that our belief measures the extent and degree of our blessing. If our belief is limited only a little can come to us, because that is as we believe. We call this the law of mental equivalents. How much life can any [of us] experience? As much as [we] can embody. There is nothing fatalistic about this. We are so constituted that we can continuously increase our embodiment. We grow in grace, as it were. We grow in power and theoretically there should be no limit to that growth. But right today we can expect to demonstrate or to have our prayers answered according to our belief and the embodiment of that belief (Holmes, 1938, p 280)."

In order for free will to exist, it had to be that we discover for ourselves, at our own pace and in our own way, how large and in what ways our unique finite container holds the Infinite. Even concepts like faith, conviction and acceptance express differently through each of us. What we embody, what our mental equivalent is about any subject, can never be compared to another. In fact, comparing ourselves to others is just another way we limit ourselves. It is through our depth of embodiment and the solidity of our personal mental equivalent that makes all the difference in whether what we desire to create demonstrates or not. This is a very personal relationship that can never be compared to another. "If prayer has been answered, it is not because God has been moved to answer one man and not another, but because one man more than another has moved himself into a right relationship with the Spirit or the Principle of Being— whichever one chooses to call It (Holmes, 1938, p 281)." This right relationship is the embodiment that we are this Infinite Intelligence.

Again, this is not "fake it till you make it". It is diving into that deeper place within all of us that already knows the Truth and immersing ourselves until it is our default way of perceiving life. When we "maintain a consistent, positive, aggressive mental attitude in the Truth," "we must sooner or later manifest according to (Holmes, 1938, p 282)" the mental equivalent we have nurtured within us. "As we bring ourselves to a greater vision, we induce a greater concept and thereby demonstrate more in our experience (Holmes, 1938, p 282)."

No matter how tough the circumstance or condition, we can always "bring ourselves to a greater vision." For, "TO DESERT THE TRUTH IN THE HOUR OF NEED IS TO PROVE THAT WE DO NOT KNOW THE TRUTH (Holmes, 1938, p 282)." "The person who can throw himself with a complete abandon into that Limitless Sea of Receptivity, having cut loose from all apparent moorings, is the one who will always receive the greatest reward (Holmes, 1938, p 282)." This takes great courage and trust. But, this trust can be built over time. We don't have to begin by cutting "loose from all apparent moorings." We can cut them one at a time. It is up to you.

"FAITH IS A MENTAL ATTITUDE WHICH IS SO CONVINCED OF ITS OWN IDEA— WHICH SO COMPLETELY ACCEPTS IT— THAT ANY CONTRADICTION IS UNTHINKABLE AND IMPOSSIBLE (Holmes, 1938, p 283)." "Unfortunately, we find [some have a] great faith in fear (Holmes, 1938, p 283)." It is up to each of us to look deeply at what we have faith in and make sure our faith serves our highest good. "We should have faith that there is but One Mind. This Mind is both the Mind of [humanity] and the Mind of God (Holmes, 1938, p 284)." So, we nurture our mental equivalent immersed in the "calm assurance", or faith, that, of course, what we know to be true is already manifested.

"Faith is not hope, it is Substance... faith may be said to be scientific, that is, we are now dealing with a Principle that has been defined and we know something about the way It works (Holmes, 1938, p 284)." We can see that if we do the work that is required of us, we will get the results that come of that work. Again, this Principle is simple, but it is not easy. How often do we find ourselves having faith in the lack of possibilities, sure that nothing can be changed or transformed? When we become conscious of these thoughts, our job is to transform them by remembering the Truth, each and every time we show faith in something that is not the Truth. "[W]e must provide different mental equivalents for healing than those which create disease (Holmes, 1938, p 285)," and remember, "faith is not a foolish fancy, it is a dynamic fact (Holmes, 1938, p 285)."

Everything hovers around the same fact; what we embody manifests. "[W]e cannot enter into peace while we are in a state of confusion. It cannot be done. We cannot manifest love when we have a mental equivalent of hate in our hearts and minds (Holmes, 1938, p 285)." The practice of Spiritual Mind Treatment may not work overnight. It may take time to rid ourselves of what we have embodied most of our lives that has gotten in our way of living the life of our dreams.

Dr. Holmes uses the example of four men looking for work, whose mental equivalents are built on the four different salaries they earned from their last jobs. "The practitioner's word... used for each in like manner but each [can] receive only [the] fill— only his mental capacity... Each attracted... , out of the Universal Good, that which he could comprehend. It is the old statement again that water will reach its own level by its own weight and without effort. So a treatment will level itself in the objective world at the level of the subjective thought and realization which projects and receives it (Holmes, 1938, p 286)."

"This does not mean that each of the above stated men will always have to receive the same compensation, for with an enlarged consciousness [or mental equivalent,] each might receive more. [Yet, a] man does not suddenly become affluent because he sits around and thinks, "I am a multi-millionaire." But when he thinks affluently he does begin to demonstrate prosperity (Holmes, 1938, p 287)."

Knowing ourselves is another key to the kingdom of creation. If we don't understand what our inner beliefs are and what we currently embody, we are creating unconsciously. This is why digging in deeply becomes important. Remember that what manifests in our lives is based on the totality of our unconscious and conscious thoughts, beliefs and embodiment. If we say over and over in our minds all day, that we are abundant, but in our hearts feel poor, very little will change in our lives. As we affirm the Truth, are we continuing to live in a rat race lifestyle? If, on the other hand, because of our affirmations, we begin to feel abundant, behave in abundant ways and challenge the old grind we have lived in, then, of course, change will occur. "Break the bonds of apparent necessity and see life as one continuous expression of the Infinite Self, and as this conception gradually dawns upon the inner thought, something will happen in the outer conditions to relieve the greater demands of necessity (Holmes, 1938, p 288)."

Never let your or anyone else's ideas about what is "realistic" get in the way of the Truth. The Truth is we are Infinite beings operating on a physical plane which is only limited by what we say it is; what we buy into as realistic. What people call realistic is the most limiting concept we have. "All cause and effect are in Spirit, they are bound together in one complete whole. One is the inside, the other the outside of the same thing (Holmes, 1938, p 289)." There is only One. We operate in and create out of this same One. This One is Infinite and everlasting. What can be bound by this? "Never let anything cause you to doubt your ability to demonstrate the Truth. CONCEIVE OF YOUR WORD AS BEING THE THING. See the desire as an already accomplished fact and rest in perfect confidence, peace and certainty, never looking for results, never wondering, never becoming anxious, never being hurried nor worried. Those who do not understand this attitude may think you are inactive but remember: "To him who can perfectly practice inaction, all things are possible" (Holmes, 1938, p 289)."

Another key is to never pray or treat for process. We must make sure we are always focused on finished results. Asking the question, "what does having this give me?" helps discover whether we are treating for result or process. If we treat for process, that process will continue and no result will become self-evident. Also, we must treat as if we have already created the result we want. "If we say, "Tomorrow it is going to be," then according to the very law we are using we hold the answer in a state of FUTURITY WHICH CAN NEVER BECOME PRESENT. If a gardener holds his seed in his hand and says, "Tomorrow I am going to plant this seed," his garden will never start growing (Holmes, 1938, p 289)."

Because there is One Mind, which includes our free will, "[n]o mistakes have been made, none are being made, and none can be made (Holmes, 1938, p 290)." Every condition, experience, decision and action that has been a part of our lives has led us to where we are now. Your life has made you into the person you are today, the one who is taking the time to read this book and transform your life. It is ours to accept the lives we have led up to this point and take responsibility in knowing we can change our lives from this moment forward. Affirm for yourself, "Everything necessary to the full and complete expression of the most boundless experience of joy is mine now." Know this, see it, feel it and BE it. Do this every day for a few minutes. We should all do this until the time comes when it is no longer necessary (Holmes, 1938, p 290)."

"If a man has had, and apparently lost, many opportunities, he must be shown that he stands at the point of limitless opportunity; that opportunity is right here today; that he sees and grasps it. It recognizes him as he recognizes it (Holmes, 1938, p 291)."
Again, it comes back to how much of this limitlessness can we embody? How large can we stretch our container to hold this endless bounty? If we are lost in thoughts of being too old, not having the skill or any other that is realistic and limiting to us creating what we want, then, we can affirm from here until our death beds and nothing will materialize. We must affirm AND dissolve those deeper beliefs that get in the way. We must let go, cut the bonds and release anything that might bind us to a belief or embodiment that is in discord with our dreams coming true.

If a practitioner is involved, "[t]he practitioner treats [for oneself], the reason being that [the] patient's mind and [the

106

practitioner's] own mind are in the One Mind (Holmes, 1938, p 291)." When a practitioner knows, this embodied Truth can be held for another. Yet, as each of us are our own container, "A word spoken in Mind will reach its own level in the objective world by its own weight; just as in physical science we know that water reaches its own level (Holmes, 1938, p 291)." Just as with the example of the four men looking for work, each will receive the results of treatment at the level of abundance their individual containers can hold. This is true for health or anything else. No matter how powerful the practitioner, the client can only receive to the level they can accept.

This is why it is not enough for a practitioner to treat for a client. For best results, the practitioner must guide the client to increase what the client believes to be possible. The client must be willing to break free of any bonds limiting what good he or she can accept and learn how to embody the same "calm assurance" held by the practitioner.

Ask the client to repeat, "There are no mistakes in the Divine Plan for me. There is no limitation, poverty, want nor lack. I stand in the midst of eternal opportunity, which is forever presenting me with the evidence of its full expression I am joy, peace and happiness. I am the spirit of joy within me. I am the spirit of peace within me, of poise and of power. I am the spirit of happiness within me. I radiate Life; I am Life. There is One Life and that Life is my life now(Holmes, 1938, p 292)."

"It is not enough to say: "There is One Life and that Life is God." We must complete this statement by saying: "That Life is my life now," because we must couple this Life with ours in order to express It. We are not becoming this Life, but are now in and of this Life. There is no other Life. God is not becoming: God IS. God is not growing; God is complete. God is not trying to find out something; God already knows (Holmes, 1938, p 292)."

Complete the treatment by saying, "In this moment my good comes to me, enough and to spare, to give and to share. I can never be exhausted, my good can never be depleted, because that Source from which my good comes is inexhaustible. Today, in this moment, the Law responds to my thought. My word is one of affirmation, rising from the knowledge that the Good, the Enduring and the True are Eternalities in my experience. I cannot be apart from that which is my good. My good is assured me by God, the Indwelling Essence of my life (Holmes, 1938, p 293)."

Chapter 18: The Law of Attraction

"Since we are thinking beings and cannot stop thinking, and since Creative Mind receives our thought and cannot stop creating, It must always be creating something for us (Holmes, 1938, p 294)." But, [t]hought can [only] attract to us that which we first mentally embody, that which has become a part of our mental make-up, a part of our inner understanding (Holmes, 1938, p 294)." Embodiment is spoken of time and time again, because it is such an important part of what we need to understand about the creative process. Once we begin to train our thoughts to focus on what we want to create, any time delay for our creation showing up in physical form has to do with the multiple layers of the unconscious, which makes up the majority of what we embody, the essence of who we are.

"As God's thought makes worlds, and peoples them with living things, so our thought makes our world and peoples it with our experiences (Holmes, 1938, p 295)." Our power to create is endless, and yet limited by what we embody as Truth. "We have thought that outside things controlled us, when all the time we have had that within which could have changed everything and given us freedom from bondage. Everyone automatically attracts to himself just what he is, and we may set it down that wherever we are, however intolerable the situation may be, we are just where we belong (Holmes, 1938, p 295)." This is why two people with the same talent can work at creating the same accomplishment and one succeeds and the other doesn't. One is not favored by God over the other and luck is not a haphazard thing. Our accomplishments are completely based on what we embody within the very essence of who we are.

"One of the ancient sayings is that "To the man who can perfectly practice inaction, all things are possible." This sounds like a contradiction until one penetrates its inner meaning, for it is only when one completely practices inaction that he arrives at the point of the true actor, for he then realizes that the act and the actor are one and the same; that cause and effect are the same; which is simply a different way of saying: "Know the truth and the truth shall make you free." (Holmes, 1938, p 295)." What Dr. Holmes means by inaction is the inner action of embodiment. We set the limitations as to what's possible for our lives. Nothing outside ourselves can limit us. Only we can do that. The deeper we understand this fact and practice affirming the Truth of our limitless being, the larger our containers grow and the more our dreams come true.

"[Y]ou never saw a successful man who went around with an atmosphere of failure (Holmes, 1938, p 296)." "The man who says of himself, "I have no personality with which to attract people," has been laboring under a delusion. He needs to be disillusioned. He must be shown that there is but One Person; this Person is manifested through every living soul. It is THE Personality. It is Complete (Holmes, 1938, p 296)." Each of us, at any moment, can tap into the One Mind that is the essence of who we are. No matter how unique our personality, it is still one with the One, thus one with everyone, thus, of course, attractive. "Nothing can hinder the man who knows that he is dealing with the One Power that creates all from Itself, moves all within Itself, and yet holds everything in its place. One with the Infinite Mind. One with the personality of God (Holmes, 1938, p 296)."

"Emerson said: "If you want a friend, be a friend." As the idea of friendship dawns upon the consciousness, the law of attraction produces friends, for one is the picture and the other is the thing (Holmes, 1938, p 297)." As we become more of a friend to ourselves, we embody friendship. As we embody friendship, friends will manifest. "[B]ut we must never think of certain people, or that a particular individual must be one of the friends, for this would be hypnotic (Holmes, 1938, p 297)," and manipulative. It is with the calm assurance that we have spoken of many times that we attract the perfect and right friends, as we deepen our relationship of friendship with ourselves. The more we deepen our self love, the more we can

110

love others. "In order to have this friendship enduring, true, worth while and a thing of beauty, we should cultivate an attitude of friendship toward everybody and everything. The one who has learned to love all people will find plenty of people who will return that love (Holmes, 1938, p 297)." "As all is Mind, and as we attract to us what we first become (Holmes, 1938, p 298)," the more we embody and express love, the more it will, of course, manifest in our lives, through wonderfully beautiful relationships that are the exact reflection of what we have become and expressed.

"Think of the whole world as your friend, but you must also be the friend of the whole world... There is always more good than bad in people, and seeing the good tends to bring it forth (Holmes, 1938, p 298)." If your tendency is to see the worst in others, it is very likely you are seeing the worst in yourself as well. Once again, we come back to what you are embodying. "Love is the grandest healing and drawing power on earth. It is the very reason for our being (Holmes, 1938, p 298)." It is only the limitations we have set for ourselves, consciously and unconsciously, that get in the way of experiencing this ultimate Truth. "[I]t is [the] law that the man who sees what he wants to see, regardless of what appears, will someday experience in the outer what he has so faithfully seen in the within (Holmes, 1938, p 298)." This is not living in denial. Very much the contrary. This is seeing the world through the eyes of Truth. Beyond all appearances, our lives work magnificently. In the greater whole, each of us has the ability to create anew in each and every moment.

Declare for yourself, "I am one with all people, with all things, with all life. As I listen in the silence, the voice of all humanity speaks to me and answers the love that I hold out to it... I give friendship and therefore I have friends. I help, therefore, I am helped. I uplift, therefore, I am uplifted. I am now surrounded by all love, all friendship, all companionship, all health, all happiness, all success. I AM ONE WITH LIFE (Holmes, 1938, p 299)."

"We mean by demonstration, bringing into our experience something which we had not experienced before; bringing it in as the result of conscious thought; and unless it is possible to do this, our whole science is a mistake and a delusion. Unless there is a Divine Principle, Universal Soul or Subjectivity, or Medium, which, of Itself— without any help or assistance— can produce things, and will, then there is nothing in this teaching. But there is a Divine Principle; and what It does for us It must do through us (Holmes, 1938, p 299)," and as us. Either this teaching is true or it isn't. There is no middle ground. Either we can create through that place of inaction, or, we can't. If we can, we can every time. And, we can, when our consciousness has fully embodied whatever it is we want to create. It is important to remember, however, that what we embody is "the sum total of [our] knowing (Holmes, 1938, p 300)." So, if while we are affirming and treating we are also doubting and being negative about what we want to create, or hold some deep belief about not getting what we want, what shows up is the totality of all of this. "[W]hen there is no longer anything in our [embodiment] which denies our word, a demonstration will be made; nothing can stop it, for the Law is Absolute (Holmes, 1938, p 300)."

"We should approach the Law normally and naturally and with a sense of ease. There is nothing peculiar or weird about it. It is a natural Law, working in a normal way, and must be thought of in this light. We should come to consider the Law and the Spirit as friends and think of them as such. In this way we shall gradually go from good to more good and from peace to greater peace. This is the natural unfoldment of Reality through man. We should EXPECT THE BEST, and so live that the best may become a part of our experience (Holmes, 1938, p 300)."

"WE MUST BE SPECIFIC IN WHAT WE DO, while at the same time never outlining how it shall be done (Holmes, 1938, p 301)." The more specific the treatment, the greater the probability that the outcome will be exactly what we wanted. But, it is important to make sure that what we are treating for is

112

an end result and not a means to an end. The Law takes care of the how. Our conscious mind is too finite to foresee the infinite possibilities of how something might come about. If we allow the Infinite Intelligence within us to lead the how, we will know when it is time to take action and what actions to take. This is what is known as Divine Guidance. It is not some greater intelligence outside of us talking through us, but our greater intelligence, one with the One Mind, which, when we listen, expands our finite mind to greater capacity and knowing. Thus, perfect and right time and action are easy to determine. "We must have a receptive and positive faith in the evidence of things not seen with the physical eye but which are eternal in the heavens (Holmes, 1938, p 301)."

"We can do more toward saving the world by proving this law than all that charity has ever given to it (Holmes, 1938, p 301)." Imagine a world where everyone embodied the Truth that "All the power of the universe is with you. Feel it, know it, and then act (Holmes, 1938, p 302)" from this place of knowing. If everyone understood this Principle, there would be no lack, thus no need to take from another. Harmony, Peace and Love would rule. Tyrants would be powerless against a race consciousness that embodied Abundance, Health, and Wholeness.

"The Universe is inexhaustible; It is limitless, knows no bounds and has no confines. We are not depending on a reed shaken by the wind, but on the Principle of Life Itself, for all that we have or ever shall need. It is not some power, or a great power, it is ALL POWER. All we have to do is to believe, never wavering, no matter what happens. As we do this, we shall find that things are steadily coming our way and that they are coming without that awful effort which destroys the peace of mind of the majority of the race. We know that there can be no failure in God's Mind, and this Mind is the Power on which we are depending (Holmes, 1938, p 302)."

"If one appears to have failed, he should realize that there are no failures in the Universe. He should completely erase the idea of failure by stating that there are no failures (Holmes, 1938, p 302)." When we label something as a failure, we have limited the Limitless Intelligence, as to how it creates what we want. The time to remember the greater good that is available to all of us is especially when what we thought we wanted doesn't show up in the form we expected. These are moments of great power. If we declare we have failed, we have set failing in motion. If we declare that there is no such thing as a failure in the Universe, and that whatever has occurred is leading us closer and closer to our success, then, it is our success that we have set in motion. "Treatment is a thing of itself; it is an entity of Infinite Intelligence, Life and Action, and nothing can hinder its operation but unbelief or a lack of adequate mental equivalents (Holmes, 1938, p 304)."

"Never depend upon people or say that things must come from this or that source. It makes no difference where things come from. SAY THAT THEY ARE, and let them come from where they may, and then if something occurs which points to a place for them to come from, it is correct to say: "If this is the place, then there is nothing which can hinder." (Holmes, 1938, p 304)." Again, we are saying stay out of the way of where and how our good comes to us. Infinite Intelligence takes care of that. It is ours to simply know our good, of course, exists. Just "Keep on [treating] until the balance of consciousness is on the affirmative side, and nothing can hinder it from demonstrating. This is inevitable for this is the way the Law operates (Holmes, 1938, p 304)."

Declare "My opportunities are unlimited… the possibilities of my experience are unlimited… today I am the instrument through which life flows (Holmes, 1938, p 304)."

"When we make a demonstration, we must take what goes with it. Therefore all demonstrations should be made in peace, confidence and joy, and in a realization of Divine Love and Perfection permeating everything. The reason for this is evident, for we are dealing with the Law of cause and effect. We are not depending upon chance but upon the Law. The

114

responsibility of setting the Law in motion is ours, but the responsibility of making It work is inherent in Its own nature. We must know that we are dealing with the Substance from which all things are made. Nothing moves but Mind, and we are dealing with the Mind that is the Mover, the Creator, the Cause of all that is or is to be. We should sense that back of the word which we speak is the Power of the Universe, surging to express Itself. Then speak the word consciously, knowing that it is Law (Holmes, 1938, p 305)."

"The limit of our ability to demonstrate depends upon our ability to provide a mental equivalent of our desires, for the law of correspondence works from the belief to the thing. But it is within our power to provide a greater mental equivalent through the unfolding of consciousness; and this growth from within will finally lead to freedom (Holmes, 1938, p 306)." As we have discussed, it is the totality of who we are that ultimately determines what we create.

This is why integrity becomes so important. Our thoughts, words and actions must all be in alignment for the Law to know what it is we truly desire. Keeping our thoughts aligned with what we desire is the first step. If we think of abundance, but speak about how we don't have enough money for what we desire, or act is if we don't have enough money, then we are out of alignment with our thoughts, words and actions and abundance will not appear. "What we demonstrate today, tomorrow and the next day, is not as important as the TENDENCY WHICH OUR THOUGHT IS TAKING ... the dominant attitude of our mind (Holmes, 1938, p 306)." When we hold a "dominant attitude" of abundance and speak and act in alignment with that attitude, abundance must ultimately appear. "As we contact this Higher Principle of our own lives— which is Perfect and Complete, needing nothing, wanting nothing, knowing everything, being happy and satisfied— and as we daily meditate upon this Indwelling God, we shall acquire a greater mental equivalent (Holmes, 1938, p 306)."

"For those who have always dwelt on limited thoughts a very good practice is to dwell upon the magnitude of the Universe. Think how many stars there are, how many fish there are in the seas, and how many grains of sand on the beaches. Think of how big the ocean is; of the immensity of space, the bigness of everything, the grandeur of everything. Mechanically, if necessary, compel the mentality to cognize Reality. Compel the consciousness to recognize Truth through reason, if no other conviction comes (Holmes, 1938, p 306)." Whatever it takes, find a way to begin impressing Truth upon you. There is no grander work to be done or a more important way to spend our time than to correct and maintain the Truth in our thoughts, words and actions.

"Our lives are the result of our self-contemplations, and are peopled with the personifications of our thoughts and ideas. Accept this without question for it is true (Holmes, 1938, p 307)." Once we accept this, it becomes much easier to recognize within ourselves that which limits us from having our dreams come true. This simple, yet earth-shattering fact, takes our focus away from the conditions and experiences in the physical world, and begins the work of re-shaping those same conditions and experiences from within the non-physical world. I am not a proponent of the Law of Attraction. I believe we create from scratch, in each moment a complete reflection of our embodiment and that it's not about attracting circumstances into our lives, but actually creating them out of the Substance that is the One Mind. The deeper we embody the calm assurance that our lives work magnificently, the more our dreams will surely be realized.

Chapter 19: Summary of Part Three: The Practice of Spiritual Mind Healing

"If there is one thing we should learn it is that spiritual treatment must not be confused with mental concentration... There is a certain mental attention we should have in giving a treatment, but this is different from the popular idea of mental concentration, as though we must hold the mind to one thought for a certain period of time (Holmes, 1938, p 308)." Once we have had the clarity, the calm assurance, that what we have treated for will manifest, we let it go and not give it another thought because we know it's already done.

The difference between having the calm assurance we keep talking about and not is this: do you ever check whether your heart is beating while you go about your day? Almost all of us would say no to this. That's because we know it's beating, we take it for granted. That's the level of knowing we want to experience around what we desire to create. Until we have that level of knowing or embodiment, we might need to keep treating.

"A conviction dawns that God is all there is (Holmes, 1938, p 309)," followed by "a series of statements— arguments perhaps— but a series of statements which finally culminate in the mental evidence being in favor of Perfect God, Perfect [Person], and Perfect Being (Holmes, 1938, p 309)." This is the heart of Spiritual Mind Treatment. Ultimately, it is not about creating stuff, but creating *who we have come here to be*. The deeper we embody the essence of the powerful, creative, spiritual beings we are, the more we uncover the "Perfect Being" or the "as me" consciousness that is our birthright.

"In mental and spiritual treatment, ... [p]ractitioner[s] endeavor... to enter into the consciousness of a state of unity of all life, in which unity exists past, present and future;... [we are] dealing not with mental suggestion but with a spiritual Presence, [we do] not seek to force an issue, but rather permit... [the] Creative Intelligence to perform a certain act (Holmes, 1938, p 309)." This Creative Intelligence is not something outside us. We are made of and create out of the same Substance, just like everything else in the Universe.

"The Bible clearly speaks of the physical universe and everything in it as though it were a word in form; that God is Spirit; that the action of Spirit upon Itself produces creation; that [we are] a complement of the Universe, an incarnation of the universe, partaking of the same nature. Consequently, [our] word is creative! This should answer the question of the students who are unable to understand how thought can become a thing; how thought can influence objective life, whether it be the physical body or the physical environment (Holmes, 1938, p 310)." We are as creative as that which we were created from. We are not just a part of God, but God Itself. If we are ever to own an "as me" consciousness this Principle must be embodied.

"Science tells us that all form comes from One Substance, made manifest through vibration. This further helps us to see the relationship of the Word to the formless, and teaches us the indestructibility and eternality of energy and cosmic stuff. The coal and oil we burn today passed, millions of years ago, from one form into another, and now, as they burn, are passing back into energy again. Nothing has happened to the energy except that it was temporarily imprisoned, that in its release and explosion it might produce heat and energy for utilitarian purposes. But nothing has happened to it (Holmes, 1938, p 311)." We are "cosmic stuff", as eternal as the Universe and as everlasting as our notion of God. Whatever God is, we are.

"We are not denying the physical universe when we seek to explain it. Physical form is real and if it were not for form, God, or Intelligence, would not be expressed (Holmes,

118

1938, p 311)." We are expressions of God expressing God. That's all there is. That's all that exists.

"Mind is individualized but never individual. This Mind which is Universal will never be any less than Universal; It will never be individual, but It will be individualized. There is a great difference. The wave in the ocean will never be a wave by itself. IT WILL BE THE OCEAN AS A WAVE (Holmes, 1938, p 312)." This analogy of the ocean is used quite often, because it is a great gift to remember in your hour of need. At any moment, no matter what the circumstance, you have the entire power of the universe and beyond within you. If you can remember this when you need it most, then you have opened yourself beyond your limitations, into the calm assurance that anything is possible.

"The Cosmic Order is the Divine Mind; the Universe in which we live is a Spiritual System; [and] we are spiritual beings... We can never change [the]Reality [of this Cosmic Order], cannot destroy It nor break Its laws; but we [limit] ourselves [in such a way] that It appears limited and unhappy and even appears to die (Holmes, 1938, p 313)." "We reproduce the Cosmos in our individual world... So every day we are living from this Unity, and projecting the experiences from it upon the screen of our objective lives. We have done this so long in ignorance that we appear to be bound by the outlines of the forms which our ignorance has projected (Holmes, 1938, p 314)." So, as we awaken from the sleep of ignorance, we free ourselves of these bonds, these illusions that we have created and create anew. We create from a greater possibility, a greater sense of wholeness and a greater sense of power.

"We seek a practical use of the Truth. The Spirit is the starting point of everything. There is a Presence in the Universe which we call God, Intelligence, Law, which by the very act of Its Word creates an objective form which is like Its Word. The Word becomes flesh. We are some part of this creative order

119

(Holmes, 1938, p 314)." But, never think that because we are some part, we are less than the whole.

"[W]e wish to demonstrate. What do we mean by demonstration? Nothing peculiar, nothing weird, nothing that pertains to ghost walking. To demonstrate means to prove, to exemplify, to manifest, to bring forth, to project into our experience something that is better than we had yesterday ... less pain, less unhappiness, less poverty, less misery, more good ... this is what is meant by a demonstration. We would like to be happier, have greater physical health. We would like to have more of what it takes to be happy, whether it be millions or marbles. These things are nothing of themselves. It is only when we think of them as entities, within themselves, that we fall down and worship them; and then that which we should possess, possesses and obsesses us. Every great spiritual genius has taught us to this effect: If you have possessions which possess you, it is better for you to lose them that you may understand their temporary, fleeting form. No great spiritual teacher has denied the advisability of using possessions (Holmes, 1938, p 314)."

Also, "It is not easy, is it, to turn from a disease and KNOW THAT THERE IS NO DISEASE, when we know very well that it is an experience of the moment. This is not easy, but the one who can do just this, can heal (Holmes, 1938, p 315)." We are not saying deny the experience. We are saying there is a greater Truth beyond the experience, beyond what we see in physical form. When we can focus on this greater Truth and raise our consciousness above the circumstance at hand, transformation and healing occur. It must, because the Law is the Law and It works absolutely. What is called for here is an unwavering stance and embodiment of the Truth, without a doubt.

We are not in competition or at odds with physicians. In fact, "It is inevitable that the day shall come when [the physician and metaphysician] will understand each other. They are working in two separate fields, which at the same time have a fundamental unity in one primal principle. But the mental and spiritual practitioner works in the field of Mind alone (Holmes, 1938, p 316)."

"[The Practitioner] starts with the premise that God is perfect, the Spiritual System is perfect, [humanity] is a part of this Spiritual System, therefore, the spiritual [person] is perfect. The practitioner does not deal with the material [person]; [but] says the spiritual [person] is perfect... If [we] were dealing directly with disease, poverty or unhappiness, [we] would be caught in its mental vibration. We should seek to disentangle our imagination from the material [person] and join it with our contemplation of the spiritual [person]. THE SPIRITUAL [PERSON] IS PERFECT. The spiritual [person] is continuously re-molding and remaking the material or physical [person]... Spirit is Timeless. Therefore the mental and spiritual practitioner must not deal with time, [but] must transcend time. Not only must [the practitioner] transcend time, but must resolutely turn away from any form of limitation (Holmes, 1938, p 317)."

"A treatment should always be definite, specific, concrete. In practical treatment one does not become subjective. The creative act is always conscious. In other words, a treatment moves in thought, sets something in motion, is an active thing (Holmes, 1938, p 318)." So, though we speak about this process as "perfect inaction," we are talking about not needing any outward action. Inwardly, practitioners are busy little bees, aligning their thoughts, words and beliefs into an alignment and embodiment that is whole and complete towards what they desire to demonstrate.

The steps of treatment are: "First, recognition (Holmes, 1938, p 318)," that all is One. "[s]econd, unification (Holmes, 1938, p 318)," which means we understand that we are this One. "We continue to do this until something comes into our consciousness which says "Yes." Then we begin the "third step: realization (Holmes, 1938, p 318)" that whatever we are treating for specifically is already accomplished in the One

121

Mind, so must certainly show up in physical form. The fourth step is gratitude for what is already done in the Mind of God. The fifth step is release. As there is nothing more for us to do, we allow the One Power, that is us and beyond us, to bring into physical form that which is already so in the One Mind. "This is what a treatment is… [W]e should be careful, after the treatment has been given, that we take no responsibility of trying to make it work. The Law will work (Holmes, 1938, p 318)." "There is a law in physics which says that water will reach its own level by its own weight. There is a law of metaphysics corresponding to it; consciousness will externalize at its own level, by its own recognition. We may call this faith, we may call it embodiment, we may call it whatever we will, there is something in the Universe which responds and corresponds to our mental states (Holmes, 1938, p 319)."

"How do we know when we have treated a patient long enough? How would one know when to stop seeing… a doctor? When [all] is well [the patient] will need no more treatments; until this time comes, treat every day for a realization of perfection (Holmes, 1938, p 319)." Each time, the practitioner releases the treatment as if it's already done. Each time the practitioner treats deepens the practitioner's embodiment of the health and wholeness, as well as for the patient, because we cannot hold a mental equivalent for someone else that is deeper and less limiting than the one we have for ourselves. "A treatment should leave the practitioner in better condition than before [the practitioner] gave it; otherwise, it is not a good treatment (Holmes, 1938, p 320)."

Some important points from Dr. Holmes to remember about treatment:

"Some think they dishonor God when they take a pill. This is superstition. Discard these thoughts and give your entire attention to realizing perfection for your patient…

Healing is not accomplished through will power but by knowing the Truth…

Limitation and poverty are not things, but are the results of restricted ways of thinking...

Law is always impersonal, neutral, receptive and reactive (Holmes, 1938, p 320)."

"A sense of separation from good causes us to feel restricted; while a sense of our Unity with GOOD changes the currents of Causation and brings a happier condition into the experience...

The same power which binds [us] will free [us] when [we] understand... the Law to be one of liberty and not of bondage...

The Law of Mind, which is the Medium of all action, is a law of perfect balance: the objective world perfectly balances the images within the subjective world. Water will reach its own level by its own weight; and according to the same law, consciousness will externalize at its own level by its own weight...

If I plant a watermelon seed, I will get watermelons, but I will get a number of melons, and they will have a lot of seeds which can produce more melons, so the thought is MULTIPLICITY but never DIVISION (Holmes, 1938, p 321)."

"The manifest universe is a result of the Self-Contemplation of God. [A person]'s world of affairs is the result of [that person's] self-contemplation...

[W]hen we know the Truth, It will compel us to act in a correct manner...

[A person], automatically and according to Law, attracts to [oneself] a correspondence of [the person's] inner mental attitudes...

Demonstration takes place through the field of the One Universal Mind. We set the Power in motion; the Law produces the effect. We plant the seed and the Law produces the plant...
Life is a mirror and will reflect back (Holmes, 1938, p 322)" what we embody.

"[A]bsolute belief in, and reliance upon, Truth... is both natural and normal (Holmes, 1938, p 322)."

"There is One Infinite Spirit and every time [a person] says "I am" [that person] proclaims It. There is One Infinite Substance and every time [we] move... [we] move... in It. There is One Infinite Law and every time [we] think... [we] set... this Law in motion...

Talk, live, act, believe and know that you are a center in this One. All the Power there is, all the Presence there is, all the Love there is, all the Peace there is, all the Good there is, and the Only God there is, is Omnipresent. Consequently, the Infinite is in and through man and is in and through everything. "Act as though I am and I will be." (Holmes, 1938, p 323)."

Chapter 20: What the Mystics Have Taught

"A mystic is not a mysterious person but is one who has a deep, inner sense of Life and of his unity with the Whole... There is nothing mysterious in the Truth, so far as It is understood, but all things seem mysterious until we understand them. A mystic is one who intuitively perceives Truth and, without mental process, arrives at Spiritual Realization (Holmes, 1938, p 327)." These are people who have a direct experience of the Divine; not just as a state of consciousness, but as a level of consciousness. They live where many of us only visit. Their day-to-day experience of life is deeply immersed in the embodiment of the One.

There are those who have had glimpses of the "direct experience of the Divine" and then proceeded to speak, paint, draw or sing about what they have seen. It is not the same as living there. But, what is important about these glimpses is that they all point to the same Truth. "[They have] revealed things that do not pass as ships in the night. [They have] revealed Eternal Verities and has plainly taught us that there is a Living Presence indwelling ALL (Holmes, 1938, p 328)."

"The mystics of every age have seen, sensed and taught THE SAME TRUTH! [They] have all sensed one identical Reality, and their testimony is in no way confusing, because the Spirit within them has borne witness to the same Truth (Holmes, 1938, p 328)." The teachings expressed in this book do not deviate from what every Mystic, or philosopher, artist or musician who has experienced the mystic state of consciousness, have expressed. "The philosophy of Jesus will remain sound when the belief in a material universe shall have been rolled up like a scroll and numbered with the things once thought to be real. So will be the philosophy of Buddha, Plato, Socrates, Emerson and Walt Whitman, and the philosophy we are writing about today (Holmes, 1938, p 329)." There is only One, thus, we are this One. This One is creative, thus we are creative. Love is the deepest message of the Divine, thus we are in alignment with the most high when we create and express ourselves from Love.

"Reason declares that that Which is Infinite cannot be divided against Itself. The Infinite is, therefore indivisible and consequently a Perfect Unit (Holmes, 1938, p 330)." In this Perfect Unit we can experience "[a]ll life... bound together by One common Law of Love, and Love is the Self-Givingness of Spirit (Holmes, 1938, p 330)." When we love ourselves with kindness and compassion, we love all beings. Just as a treatment on ourselves treats the All, so does Love.

"In treatment there should always be a recognition of the absolute Unity of God and [humanity]: the Oneness, Inseparability, Indivisibility, Changelessness. God as the big circle and [humanity] as the little circle. [Humanity] is in God and God is [humanity], just as a drop of water is in the ocean, while the ocean is the drop of water (Holmes, 1938, p 331)." Once again, our favorite metaphor is reinforced. It is not narcissistic to love and accept ourselves. It is the essence of loving all of life. It is the mental equivalent necessary to love another. Our limitation to loving others starts with our limitation to loving ourselves. Mystics through the ages have taught and continue to teach that there is no separation. The deeper we can embody this Truth the more we can feel the "Self-Givingness" reaching out through the Infinite embedded in each of us.

"We came from Life and are in Life, so we are One with Life; and we know that Instinctive Life within— which has brought us to the point of self-recognition— still knows in us the reason for all things, the purpose underlying all things; and we know that there is nothing in us of fear, doubt or confusion which can hinder the flow of Reality to the point of our recognition. We are guided daily by Divine Intelligence into paths of peace, wherein the soul recognizes its Source and meets It in joyful union, in complete At-One-ment (Holmes, 1938, p 331)." It is through our willingness to stay in treatment as long as it takes to experience this "At-One-ment" that makes all the difference. When we first start doing spiritual mind treatments, and using the language of Oneness, the "self-recognition" that Dr. Holmes speaks of, may not be readily apparent. But, through practice and persistence, a sense of Unity will begin to sink in. Mystics tell us that a practice of meditation or contemplation is required to feel the gentle nudge of the Divine. Sit quietly until your thoughts of discord rest. It is at that point that a sense of At-One-ment becomes self-evident.

"The Unity of Good is a revelation of the greatest importance, for it teaches us that we are One with the Whole and One with each other. The… actual [Family of Humanity] will be made apparent on earth to the degree that [we] realize… true Unity (Holmes, 1938, p 332)." The deeper our practice the more we become a model for others to practice. Mystics inspire us through the actual demonstration of their lives, being peaceful and in loving harmony with the Divine. We can spark others by standing as model for Unity as well.

"The higher the sense of Truth, the greater will be the realization of the uniqueness of individual character and personality (Holmes, 1938, p 332)." This is the most fantastic paradox of all. The more we recognize our Oneness, the more freedom we feel to express our uniqueness, not from a sense of revolution or rebellion, but from a center of Love. The deeper we tap into Infinite Intelligence, the more our talents and gifts express themselves, for the good of all, in a way that only we, as an individuation of the One, can express. "Individuality means self-choice, volition, conscious mind, personified Spirit, complete freedom and a Power to back up that freedom (Holmes, 1938, p 332)." So, being One does not mean we all the same— quite the contrary. We are all made out of the same God; yet God expresses uniquely and magnificently as each of us. The mystics teach us that when we celebrate our diversity, we celebrate the infinite number of ways God can show up.

"The great mystics have all agreed that [a person]'s life is his [or hers] to do with as [that person] chooses, but that when [we] turn… to the One, [we] will always receive inspiration from on High (Holmes, 1938, p 333)." Because of God's individuation through each of us, we all have a unique relationship with our Divine center. We invent different names, different rituals, and different ways of communicating with our higher selves. "THE INFINITE IS PERSONAL TO EVERY SOUL WHO BELIEVES IN THE INFINITE (Holmes, 1938, p 334)." So, the words and ways in which spiritual mind treatment works for one person can be very different from another. Neither is right nor wrong. What matters is that whatever words and feelings we invoke gives us an experience of the Divine. The goal is to commune with that part of ourselves that knows we are One with the One Mind. We may look to others for guidance in how they do it, but, ultimately, each of us must find our own way.

"One of the most illuminating things which mysticism has revealed is that evil is not an ultimate reality, it is simply an experience of the soul on its journey toward Reality (Holmes, 1938, p 335)." The fact the evil is not an ultimate Reality does not mean we don't experience evil as such. It simply reminds us that "It is not a thing of itself but simply a misuse of power (Holmes, 1938, p 335)." Because we have free will, we can use our Power anyway we wish. The Law is impersonal and does not judge what we ask of it. It only says, "Yes." But, what appears as evil can only exist in an unconscious world.

As stated earlier in the book, there is less barbarism throughout humanity, per capita, than at any other point in history. More and more people are listening to the gentle nudge of the Divine Guidance that is built into all of us. It is up to those of us who have already heard and followed that nudge of Love to hold the Truth for the rest of humanity, knowing the inevitability of everyone evolving to where Love and Harmony are the defaults in all people, throughout the world.

"Some day we shall learn to lay our burdens on the altar of Love, that they may be consumed by the fire of faith in the Living Spirit (Holmes, 1938, p 335)." "Our individualized Universe is forever complete, yet forever completing Itself, in order that every experience may teach us to transcend some previous one, in ever ascending cycles, upward bound (Holmes, 1938, p 336)." Quantum physics teaches us that in each moment, we perceive a Universe that has materialized from an endless amount of possibilities that existed before we perceived it. We do this again and again. If our conscious awareness does not evolve, what we materialize is pretty much the same as the moment before. But, if we can imagine and embody a different perception, it is this new perception which will appear. "IN SUCH DEGREE AS WE CONTEMPLATE THE SPIRIT OF LIVINGNESS, IT BECOMES MANIFEST... Thus our recognition of It becomes Its recognition of us at the level of our recognition of It (Holmes, 1938, p 336)."

"NO DEVIL, NO HELL, NO TORMENT, NO DAMNATION outside of one's own state of thought, NO PUNISHMENT outside of that self-inflicted, through ignorance; and NO SALVATION OUTSIDE OF CONSCIOUS CO-OPERATION WITH THE INFINITE. Heaven and Hell are states of consciousness (Holmes, 1938, p 337)." It is ours and ours alone to stop punishing ourselves, limiting ourselves and tormenting ourselves. When our own minds drive us crazy, that is the perfect time to treat and re-connect to the calm assurance of our Oneness with the Divine. When we feel urgent, out of step, out of sorts or in any way in discord with the One Mind, no matter what the circumstance, that is the time to sit quietly and rediscover who we truly are.

"Evolution is the awakening of the soul to a recognition of its unity with the Whole. Material evolution is an effect, not a cause... The man Jesus became the Christ through a complete realization of the Unity of Spirit and the Absoluteness of His word (Holmes, 1938, p 337)." And thus, we return to the great paradox, because "The most precious thing a [person] possesses is [one's] own individuality; indeed, this is the only

129

thing [we] really [have], or [are]. For one instant to allow any outside influence to enter or control this individuality is a crime against [our] real self (Holmes, 1938, p 338)." We deepen our sense of the One, and find the inspiration that fires our unique gifts into being. "The time has come in our evolution when we should awaken to the recognition that behind each one stands the Eternal Mind— that each has complete access to It; that each may come to It for inspiration and revelation— and that surrounding all is a Divine Law obeying the dictates of this Eternal Mind (Holmes, 1938, p 339)."

"Every time one conceives an idea, it is God expressing (Holmes, 1938, p 339)" as God. Even evolution is a conceived idea. "Evolution, then, is not a thing in itself; it is an effect (Holmes, 1938, p 340)." It is because we have free will that evolution becomes necessary. "It seems as though behind evolution there is an irresistible pressure, compelling more, better, higher and greater things (Holmes, 1938, p 340)." The gentle nudge towards Love and Harmony, built into the very fabric of the Universe, comes to us at the pace we allow and are willing to listen. "When we know enough to multiply the loaves and fishes, we shall do so. When we know enough to walk on the water, we shall be able to do that and it will all be in accordance with natural law in a spiritual world (Holmes, 1938, p 341)."

"The mystic intuitively perceives Truth, and often without any process of reasoning— immediately is aware, with what Swedenborg called a sort of "interior awareness," a spiritual sense. There can and does descend into our minds— embody and personify in our person— a Divinity, a Unity, the Spirit of God, the direct incarnation of the Original Thing, in us— the mystical presentation of Christ (Holmes, 1938, p 341)." It doesn't matter which religion or philosophy we may believe in, "Buddha, Jesus, Plato, Socrates, Aristotle, Swedenborg, Emerson, Whitman, Browning or any of the other great mystics, no matter in what age they have lived, [found] the same Ultimate (Holmes, 1938, p 342)."

"Mystics have felt this wonderful Power working from within; and have responded to It; and as certain evidence that they were not laboring under delusions, THEY HAVE ALL SENSED THE SAME THING. Had the impressions been psychic only, each would have seen and sensed a different thing, for each would merely have been seeing through the darkness of his own subjective mentality (Holmes, 1938, p 342)." This is an important difference to reemphasize between psychic abilities and intuition. Psychic abilities are taking impressions that are in the One Mind, and trying to make sense of them through our individual personalities. Some folks are better at that than others and interpretations on those impressions can vary widely. Intuition is listening directly to what the One Mind tells us about our relationship to it and, as Dr. Holmes has stated, every Mystic throughout the ages has interpreted this the same. "Illumination will come as [we] more and more realize... Unity with the Whole, and as [we] constantly endeavor to let the Truth operate through [us] (Holmes, 1938, p 343)."

"The highest... practice is to listen to this Inner Voice and to declare Its Presence. The greater a man's consciousness of this Indwelling I AM, the more fully he will live. This will never lead to illusion, but will always lead to Reality (Holmes, 1938, p 344)." Whenever someone expresses themselves as being realistic, they are talking about their limited perception of what is Reality. It is never the Truth. Truth is only Truth if it roots all the way down and the only Truth at the root is that of Love, Harmony and Wholeness. Any discord we may be experiencing cannot be rooted in the Truth. It may appear real. We may even experience its physicalness. But, if we are open to the "highest... practice" we will ultimately experience a life filled with Truth. "All mystics have seen this Cosmic Light. This is why it is said they were illumined (Holmes, 1938, p 344)."

"If a spiritual treatment could be seen (and a spiritual treatment merely means the mind unifying with Good) it would be seen as a pathway of light... In moments of deepest realization, the great mystics have sensed that One Life flows through all, and that all are some part of that Life. They have also seen Substance, a fine, white, brilliant stuff, forever falling into everything; a Substance indestructible and eternal. It is at such times of complete realization that they have been blinded by the LIGHT of which we have been speaking (Holmes, 1938, p 345)." This metaphor can only carry us so far, because what we seek is not a blinding by the light, but an awakening of the heart that is useful and applicable in our daily lives. "How are we going to make this practical, other than feeling this in our meditation for practical work, for healing, for demonstration? This is what we mean by a method, a procedure, a technique and a realization: that accompanying the method and technique should always come as much of the realization as we can generate at that time (Holmes, 1938, p 346)." This is the practice of the Mystics through the ages, available to each of us, today.

Chapter 21: Some Phases of the Subjective Life

"We do not have two minds, but we do have... dual aspect[s]... in what we call the objective and subjective states of consciousness. The objective mind is that part... which functions consciously. It is the part of us which is self-knowing and without it we would not be self-conscious entities. Our conscious mind is the place where we consciously live and are aware that we are living... Our subjective mind is our... emanation in Universal Subjectivity... We certainly do not wish to deviate from that which psychology teaches about the mind... in its conscious, subconscious, or subjective states. We merely wish to add this: the reason we have a subjective mind is that Subjectivity existed in the Universe prior to our use of It; and where we use It, It forms around us a subjective personification of ourselves, which is a result of the action and the reaction of our (Holmes, 1938, p 347)" embodiment. The Universal Subjectivity is the creative force of the One Mind, which is constantly creating everything that exists in physical form every moment of every day.

The important thing to understand here is that what is created is not permanent, but being created and recreated all the time. This is why what we embody is so powerful. If at any moment, what we embody changes, so does the physical form we call our lives. Remember, what we embody is not just our thoughts and beliefs, but the totality of what we have arrived at as our perception of reality, which includes the influence we have allowed from others.

"Race-suggestion is a very real thing, and each individual carries around with him (and has written into his mentality) many impressions which he never consciously thought of or experienced (Holmes, 1938, p 348)." The easiest way to recognize this are the rules we follow simply because everybody else we know follows them. But, some of the ways we are affected by race consciousness that are harder to

133

detect, have to do with what we believe to be realistic or how certain diseases are believed to affect us.

When somebody with cancer has a healing that cannot be explained medically, it's called a miracle, when in fact, it is simply the person embodying a belief that is beyond the race consciousness of what is believed to be possible. Race consciousness once believed that no one could run a mile in under four minutes. The first person to do so was the first person to embody a consciousness that said it was possible.

"Just as each person, place or thing has a subjective atmosphere or remembrance, so each town, city or nation has its individual atmosphere... The combined thought of those who inhabit a nation creates a national consciousness which we speak of as the psychology of that people (Holmes, 1938, p 348)." So, the paradox of the One Mind and our Individuation of the One Mind, which is incredibly powerful when held consciously, if held unconsciously, leads to "a tendency, on the part of all of us, to reproduce the accumulated subjective experiences of the human race (Holmes, 1938, p 349)."

One of the best examples in which the paradox of the One Mind and our Individuation of the One Mind is used consciously and powerfully is when "anyone who is sympathetically inclined toward the race, or vibrates to the race-thought, might pick up the entire race-emotion and experience and— if [they] were able to bring it to the surface— [and] consciously depict it. Many of the world's orators, actors and writers have been able to do this (Holmes, 1938, p 349)."

"There is, of course, a much deeper seat of knowledge than the subjective mind, which is the Spirit; direct contact with the Spirit is Illumination (Holmes, 1938, p 350)." This is what the Mystics throughout the ages have experienced and shared with humanity. This is the message of Truth that never changes. This is the gentle nudge towards Wholeness, Peace, Harmony and Love.

"Each person has a mental atmosphere which is the result of all that he has thought, said and done, and consciously or unconsciously perceived (Holmes, 1938, p 350)." This is what I have labeled throughout this book as embodiment. "No matter what the lips may be saying, the inner thought outspeaks them, and the unspoken word often carries more weight than the spoken (Holmes, 1938, p 350)." This is why it's so important to dig deep within ourselves and uncover anything that might be in discord with our true desires and with our true selves.

Another aspect of race consciousness and the One Mind is the idea of mental telepathy. "The main fact to emphasize is that mental telepathy would not be possible, unless there were a medium through which it could operate. This medium is Universal Mind, and it is through this medium, or avenue, that all thought-transference, or mental telepathy, takes place (Holmes, 1938, p 350)." Those people who have some ability to tap into the part of the One Mind, which holds every thought ever thought by anyone ever, "we call psychics, but all people are really psychic, since all have a soul or subjective mind… Whatever may have happened at any time on this plane remains within its subjective atmosphere as a memory picture of the experiences of those who have lived here. These pictures, or vibrations, may be clearly discerned by those who can read them (Holmes, 1938, p 351)."

Thus, psychic ability is available to anyone who is open and wants to read the pictures or vibrations. Like anything else in life, we must first believe it is possible. Once we believe in the One Mind and recognize Its Infinite Nature, this is a pretty easy step to take. "We need not be astonished when a psychic gives us the complete history of our family, even to reciting the things that engaged the attention of our ancestors while they were on earth. The psychic is merely reading from the subjective remembrance (Holmes, 1938, p 352)."

This must not be confused with intuition. As we have defined earlier in this book, intuition is the mystic ability to go deeper than the race memories that a psychic is interpreting, to the One Truth that rests at the center of all being. Intuition does not predict the future or call forth the past, but is in the present moment. It guides us each step of the way, towards a greater and greater fulfillment of our reason for being. It is an unwavering knowing of our unique and magnificent expression of the Divine and what steps are ours to take to achieve what is ours to do.

"A psychic can enter the stream of thought of anyone whose vibration he can mentally contact, be that person in the flesh or out of it; and since we are all psychic— all having a soul element— we are all doubtless communicating with each other to the degree that we sympathetically vibrate toward each other... This is why we often feel uneasy in the presence of certain people, or when we mentally contact some condition and are aware of a disturbed inner feeling, without any apparent reason (Holmes, 1938, p 353)."

So, when we talk about prophesy, "any incident which has transpired in the past is an active thing in the present, unless the vibration is neutralized, when it no longer has existence anywhere (Holmes, 1938, p 353)." "The continuation of the past, through the present, into the future, is a movement of causation passing from cause to effect; and because the movement is first set in motion in a field of Mind which is purely subjective, both cause and effect will exist at any point during the sequence of this movement. The clairvoyant vision, then, contacting it at any point— even before the final outcome— will see the final outcome. There is nothing fatalistic about this. A thing can appear to be fatalistic without necessarily being so. This we should understand, because the human mind in its ignorance has created great psychic laws for itself. Therefore, if one has been told anything in the way of a prophecy which is negative, it should be directly refuted (Holmes, 1938, p 354)." This is the power of Spiritual Mind Treatment.

We may let a psychic influence us to create the outcome he or she has prophesied, but then *we* did that. It is the same as a doctor saying we have terminal cancer. Those that survive are able to embody a different reality from the one presented to them by the doctor. "EVERY THOUGHT SETS THE FULFILLMENT OF ITS DESIRE IN MOTION IN MIND, AND MIND SEES THE THING AS ALREADY DONE! Mental tendencies set in motion cast their shadows before, and a psychic often sees the complete manifestation of an idea before it has had time to materialize in the objective world. This is what constitutes the average spirit of prophecy, for prophecy is the reading of subjective tendencies and seeing them as already accomplished facts (Holmes, 1938, p 355)." In the end, we must remember that we source the outcome in our lives. No one can do that for us.

Chapter 22: Finding the Christ

"Who is Christ? The Son, begotten of the only Father—not the "only begotten Son of God." ... This world forms and disintegrates, as the body does, but creation goes on forever. Therefore, the Eternal is forever begetting that which is the realization of Its own perfection (Holmes, 1938, p 357)." The Christ consciousness is "where a sense of the Oneness of all Life so enters [our] being that there is no sense of otherness. It is here that the mentality performs seeming miracles, because there is nothing to hinder the Whole from coming through. We can do this only by providing the mental equivalents of Life, by dwelling and meditating upon the immensity of Life and the fact that, as vast, as immense, as limitless as It is, the whole of It is brought to the point of our own consciousness. We comprehend the Infinite only to the degree that It expresses Itself through us, becoming to us that which we believe It to be. So we practice daily in our meditations the realization of Life: "Infinite, indwelling Spirit [as] me, Almighty God [as] me, Real Substance [as] me, that which is Truth [as] me (Holmes, 1938, p 358)."

"Right here, through our own nature, is the gateway and the path which leads to illumination, to realization, to inspiration, to the intuitive perception of everything. The highest faculty in [us] is intuition and it comes to a point sometimes where, with no process of reasoning at all, [we] instantly know... (Holmes, 1938, p 358)." Once we are able to stand in the Truth without wavering, we will be able to heal the sick, walk on water and feed the masses with but five loaves of bread and two fish. But, even if we do waver, the more we are willing to remember and return to our stand in the Truth, the more loving, kind and compassionate our lives will be.

"We must understand the Christ is not a person, but a Principle... Jesus the man became a living embodiment of the Christ. If we can look upon Jesus from this viewpoint, we shall

139

be able to study his life as a living example. What is more inspiring than to contemplate the consciousness of a man who has the faith to stand in front of a paralyzed man and tell him to get up and walk, and to know very well that he is going to get up and walk; or to stand in front of the tomb of a dead man and tell him to come forth (Holmes, 1938, p 359)!"

"Jesus never thought of himself as different from others. His whole teaching was that what he did, others could do. He located God and the Kingdom of Heaven within himself. He had plunged beneath the material surface of creation and found its Spiritual Cause (Holmes, 1938, p 361)." If we are willing to do the same, "plunge beneath the material surface of creation," we too, will find "its Spiritual Cause." The symbolism behind his forty days in the desert is key here. Just as the caterpillar must go into the cocoon to become the butterfly, we must be willing to go into our darkest places alone to come out filled with the Christ consciousness. Speaking the words of an affirmative prayer or spiritual mind treatment is certainly helpful, but this won't do it alone. We have to be willing to go as deep as it takes within ourselves to experience ourselves as the One Mind. When Dr. Holmes speaks of the steps of treatment, he says very clearly that we must not leave step one, Recognition that there is only One, and step two, Unification or our knowing that we are this One, before we fully experience ourselves as the One Mind. Otherwise, step three, Affirmation, will not have the desired power necessary to create. "[H]ow few has come the real Truth— the realization that God is indwelling in the soul and spirit of man! And yet this realization is what gave Jesus his wonderful power (Holmes, 1938, p 362)."

"The nearer consciousness comes to this Truth, the more Cosmic sweep it has, the more power it has (Holmes, 1938, p 362)." This is why our lives improve by the exact increments of our embodiment of the Truth. Because, "Christ is not limited to any person, nor does He appear in only one age (Holmes, 1938, p 363)," we do not have to be Jesus to experience the magnificent Power that is available to us. We have within us everything necessary to become the Christ as

140

fully as Jesus did. It is certainly in our realm of possibility, but, even if we embody a little of this incredible Infinite Intelligence, our lives will demonstrate a beauty and magnificence we have not before accomplished.

"Our conscious intelligence is as much of Life as we understand... What is it we need for greater freedom? Nothing but a greater realization of what we already know (Holmes, 1938, p 364)." Because we have free will, it is left up to us to uncover that part of ourselves and realize the Wholeness, Peace, Poise and Power we truly are. "Others can treat us; they can set the Law in motion for us and help us to become prosperous. This is both good and helpful, but the evolution of the individual— the unfoldment of personality, the enlightenment of the soul, the illumination of the spirit— can come only to the degree that the individual himself purposes to let Life operate through him (Holmes, 1938, p 364)."

"The answer to every question is within [us], because [we are] within Spirit, and Spirit is an Indivisible Whole! The solution to every problem is within [us]; the healing of all disease is within [us]; the forgiveness of all sin is within [us]; the raising of the dead is within [us]; Heaven is within [us]... God is the Infinite Spirit, the Limitless Conscious Life of the Universe... The One Indivisible Whole (Holmes, 1938, p 365)." Make it your daily practice to uncover more and more of the "One Indivisible Whole" that is within and without. "Jesus spent much of his time communing with his own soul, for it is through our inner [work] that we contact (Holmes, 1938, p 366)" the part of ourselves that knows the Truth and opens us to the Divine Guidance that is always available. "Call it conscience, intuition, or what we will, it is there. No man need go unguided through life, for all are divine at the center and all are Images of the Most High (Holmes, 1938, p 367)!"

"To think of Jesus as being different from other men is to misunderstand his mission and purpose in life. He was a way-shower, and proved his way to be a correct one! His method was direct, dynamic, and powerful, yet extremely easy and

141

simple to comprehend. He believed in God in himself, as Power and Reality. Believing in God within, he was compelled to believe in himself. To the illumined, has ever come self-realization and I-AM-NESS (Holmes, 1938, p 367)." Many of us have moments of awareness of our "I-AM-NESS," as a state of consciousness, that dissolves away and we are left with a more mundane perception of ourselves and life. What Jesus accomplished was a level of consciousness where he lived, not just visited. That possibility to live in an "I-AM_NESS" state of consciousness is within each of us.

The more we take time to visit this "I-AM-NESS" state of consciousness, the more we build our home there with our focus and attention. Over time, it is our old ways of perceiving the world and ourselves that dissolve away as we become stronger in our stance in the One as our home. "Jesus spoke from the heights of spiritual perception, proclaiming the deathless reality of the individual life, the continuity of the individual soul, the unity of Universal Spirit within [everyone and every being]... He proclaimed his divinity through his humanity and taught that all men are brothers (Holmes, 1938, p 368)."

"To realize within oneself a divine Presence, a perfect Person, is to recognize the Christ... Let us learn to be still and let the Truth speak through us; to be still and know that the inner light shines... The Christ knows that His individuality is indestructible; that He is an eternal Being, living forever... The Christ rises from the ashes of human hopes, pointing the way to a greater realization of life... We are never left without a witness of the Eternal, and in our greatest moments— in those flash-like visions of mystic grandeur— we know that we are made of eternal stuff, fashioned after a Divine Pattern (Holmes, 1938, p 369)."

Chapter 23: Immortality

In this chapter, Dr. Holmes speaks on his views on immortality, which, to be candid, I am somewhat uncomfortable with. To be complete in these being "Cliff Notes", I will include the basics of what he is saying. I will begin by speaking to my beliefs on the subject as these are even more so, "Cliff's Notes."

Whether we are immortal in totality or not should not dissuade us from making full use of our time on earth in the physical bodies we have presently. The teachings in this book are about maximizing our Divine potential in *this* physical lifetime. It is most important to me that we focus on that. Buddhists tell us that reincarnation is a fact, but place emphasis on the importance of living *this* life, in *this* moment, well. They constantly remind us that we are going to die, that life is short, and so they encourage us to spend it in kindness and compassion. With this in mind, I found the following quotes best explain Dr. Holmes' position on immortality.

"To most of us, immortality means that we shall persist after the experience of physical death, retaining a full recognition of ourselves, and having the ability to recognize others. If our full capacities go with us beyond the grave, we must be able to think consciously, to will, to know and to be known, to communicate and to receive communications. We must be able to see and be seen, to understand and to be understood. In fact, if one is really to continue as a self-conscious personality beyond this life, he can do so only if he maintains a continuous stream of the same consciousness and self-knowingness that he now possesses (Holmes, 1938, p 371)."

"Individuality might remain without remembrance, but not so with personality for what we are is the result of what we have been, the result of what has gone before (Holmes, 1938,

143

p 372)." Strange as it may seem, we do not have the same physical bodies that we had a few months ago, they have completely changed. New particles have taken the place of the old, and the only reason that they have taken the same form is that something within has provided the same mold. Our bodies are like a river, forever flowing. The Indwelling Spirit alone maintains the identity (Holmes, 1938, p 374)."

"The soul needs a physical body here, else it would not have evolved one. But when by reason of disease, decay or accident the physical body is no longer an adequate instrument through which the soul may function, it lays the present body aside and continues to function through a more subtle one. When we pass from this plane, shall we become spirits or shall we have tangible bodies? Form is necessary to self-expression. We reiterate, there can be no consciousness without something of which to be conscious (Holmes, 1938, p 374)."

"If the soul can create and sustain a body here, there is no reason to deny its ability to create and sustain one hereafter! ... we might have a body within the physical one, which could be as real as the one of which we are accustomed to think (Holmes, 1938, p 375)."

"The "resurrection body," then, will not be snatched from some Cosmic Shelf, as the soul soars aloft. It is already within and we may be certain that it will be a fit instrument for the future unfoldment of the soul... It would seem, then, that we have a spiritual body now, and need not die to receive one. We now remember the past, and have outlived many physical bodies during this life. So it looks as if we were already immortal and need not die to take on immortality (Holmes, 1938, p 376)."

"TO KNOW THAT WE MAINTAIN AN IDENTITY INDEPENDENT OF THE PHYSICAL BODY IS PROOF ENOUGH OF IMMORTALITY (Holmes, 1938, p 377)."

"It seems logical to infer that in providing for the continuity of life and the triumphant progression of the soul, Nature has endowed us with duplicate senses that we may be able to reproduce our entire life, with all of its action and reaction, on another plane (Holmes, 1938, p 378)."

"I believe that we often do communicate with the subjectivity of those who are departed, whether they know we are doing so or not; but the messages that come in our present state of evolution are very incoherent (Holmes, 1938, p 380)."

At this point in the chapter, Dr. Holmes discusses reward and punishment which are important topics in their impact on what we create in our lives. If we feel punished, we are the ones punishing ourselves. So it is the same with reward. "Life is a blessing or a curse, according to the use we make of it. In the long run, no one judges us but ourselves and no one condemns us but ourselves... We are our own reward and our own punishment... No one gives to us but ourselves and no one robs us but ourselves. We need not fear either God or the devil. There is no devil, and God is Love... Every [person] is an incarnation of God... We should neither be disturbed by the wailing of prophets, nor the anathemas of theology. We cannot believe that because we have subscribed to some creed, we have thereby purchased a seat in heaven, nor can we believe in any vindictive or malicious power in the universe, which damns us because we have erred through human ignorance (Holmes, 1938, p 383)." The only reward or punishment that exists in the Universe is the one we embody and, thus, bring in to form. We are at choice. We are always at choice.

And here, we re-enter the world of the hereafter, which, as I have stated, should not take away from focusing on the here and now.

"We shall continue in our own individual stream of consciousness but forever and ever expanding. Not less but ever more: more and still more ourselves... We confidently

145

expect to meet friends who are on the other side, and to know and be known (Holmes, 1938, p 384)."

I believe in the continuation of the personal life beyond the grave, in the continuity of the individual stream of consciousness with a full recollection of itself and the ability to know and to make itself known (Holmes, 1938, p 385)."

"Time heals all wounds, adjusts conditions, explains facts; and time alone satisfies the expanding soul, reconciling the visible with the invisible (Holmes, 1938, p 387)." I feel comfort from such a statement. For, "When we meet each other, do we not feel that subtle Presence which flows through all things and gives light and color to our everyday experiences? In our own souls, in the silent processes of thought and understanding, do we not sense another Presence? There is something Divine about us which we have overlooked. There is more to us than we realize (Holmes, 1938, p 388)." In that recognition of Presence, in that realization of the Divine, time stands still and we are immortal.

Chapter 24: General Summary

These final statements from Dr. Holmes are brilliant. As is true with the rest of the book, I have picked out the quotes that resonate with me the most. For many, my choice of quote is my commentary. Where I thought I could add something, I have. Otherwise, I have simply left his quotes to stand on their own.

"The Mind of [humanity] is... the Mind of God, therefore it contains within itself unlimited possibility of expansion and self-expression. The conscious mind of [each of us] is self-knowing, self-assertive; it has volition, will, choice and may accept or reject (Holmes, 1938, p 390)."

"[T]he mind of [humanity] is as infinite as is [our] capacity to understand [our] true relationship to God or Spirit. The mind of [humanity] is continuously unfolding into a greater recognition of its real plan in the creative order of the Universe (Holmes, 1938, p 390)."

"Spirit is really the only Mind there is. It is Eternal. It never began nor will It ever cease to be. It is complete and perfect... [It] is the only Conscious Intelligence in the Universe. Therefore It is the only Directive Intelligence in the Universe. Because the mind of [humanity] is the Mind of God in [each of us], [our minds are] conscious and directive. It is to [us] what God is to the Universe (Holmes, 1938, p 390)."

"The conscious mind of [humanity] is that part of, or unity with, the Supreme Spirit which enables [each of us] to be an individual unit, separate in identity without becoming separated from, the Whole Spirit of God, the Whole Mind of God (Holmes, 1938, p 391)." This is the beautiful paradox we spoke of earlier in the book. The more we recognize our unity in the One, the greater our power to express our individuation of that One. "The Eternal has placed [Itself] at the center of [our] being in order that [we] may function individually. The discovery of this, the greatest truth about [us], is the greatest discovery of the ages (Holmes, 1938, p 391)."

"The Universal Subjectivity is... [a] creative, universal energy waiting to be used, to be operated upon. Willing, but having no volition of Its own. Ready, but having no initiative. Formless, but ready to take form... Mind in Its subjective state cannot act until It is set in motion by mind in a conscious state... [We call] It forth into expression (Holmes, 1938, p 392)."

"In Universal Mind is contained the essence of everything that ever was, is or shall be... The correct understanding that Mind in Its unformed state can be called forth into individual use is the key to all proper mental and spiritual work from a practical viewpoint. To know that we are surrounded by such a creativeness is not enough, however, we must use this knowledge for definite purposes if we expect to make conscious use of the law for personal self-expression (Holmes, 1938, p 392)."

"No form is permanent. All forms return into the Formless. The Formless is Eternal. All form is temporary. [This] is [the] eternal play of Life upon Itself (Holmes, 1938, p 393)." Even stars and galaxies are not infinite. Everything transforms, eventually, within the Infinite Intelligence that is always and everlasting.

"This Limitless Medium we may use for whatsoever purpose we will. If we use It for destructive purposes we shall bring destruction upon ourselves. The Universe is fool proof (Holmes, 1938, p 394)." The Universe finds Its own balance and can never be out of balance, in just the same way water finds its own level. The deeper we embody and align ourselves with this Truth, the deeper we can embody our own balance and have it take shape as our experience in our lives. "We can use this power for the healing of the physical body or for the changing... of conditions around us... [Our] mind is the Mind of God functioning at the level of [our] understanding of [our] place

148

in the Universe. [We contact] the Mind of God at the center of [our] own being (Holmes, 1938, p 394)."

"This Law of Mind is [our] access to the Original Creative Genius of the Universe, and has no intention for us other than the intention that we give It... A perfect cause must produce a perfect effect. The normal functions of life are harmonious but we interfere with these in our ignorance and thus bring discord into temporary being (Holmes, 1938, p 394)." It is the totality of what we embody as true that creates the life experience we have. It is not enough to change our thinking, though that is an excellent start. We must dig down into the recesses of our being and root out any weeds that are not steeped in Truth, until all that is left within us is the Truth. It is at this point that ignorance is obliterated and discord disappears. "The cosmic engine is started but [we] guide... it in [our] own [lives]. It goes for [us] in the direction in which it is driven. This driving is not by force but by agreement, unification and acquiescence. We must believe. On this hangs all the law and the prophets (Holmes, 1938, p 395)." "[The Law] is a mirror and a perfect one (Holmes, 1938, p 396)." Whatever we embody turns into physical form instantly.

"The nature of Reality is such that Universal Mind has unlimited power but so far as [we are] concerned It has only the power which [we give] to It. [We give] It [the same] power when we say], "I am weak, sick or unhappy (Holmes, 1938, p 396)," as when we say "I am healthy, whole and complete." Each of us puts forth what we embody about ourselves. This is why it is so important to particularly watch our "I AM" statements. How we define ourselves feeds the Law and returns to us that which we have fed It.

"The Law of Mind obeys the orders that are given It whether we are conscious or unconscious that such orders are being given. Being entirely sensitive to [what we embody] and by its very nature absolutely receptive as well as intelligent and responsive to it— and at the same time being creative— it is easy to see what a tremendous power we have at our conscious disposal... Always remember that you are not dealing with a reluctant Force but with a completely receptive one which, by Its very nature, is compelled to receive the images of your thought (Holmes, 1938, p 397)."

"When we treat we should be specific. "Whatsoever things we desire" when we pray we should "believe that we have them." This is the whole secret, a complete... acceptance and embodiment of our desires (Holmes, 1938, p 398)." We "believe that we have them," because as we create the mental equivalent in ourselves, in the invisible, we do have them. The deeper we accept our having what we desire as fact, the stronger the power to bring it into physical form. "Our mental acceptances should be filled with conviction, warmth, color and imagination. The creative power responds to feeling more quickly than to any other mental attitude. Therefore we should try to feel the reality of what we are doing when we give a treatment. This reality is felt as we become more and more convinced that Spirit responds to us (Holmes, 1938, p 398)."

"[God] is the very breath of our breath ... the imagination back of our word. It is the creative power in our thought and the law and energy that executes that thought. "God is all in all, over all and through all." (Holmes, 1938, p 398)."

"If [we] make a complete mental picture of [ourselves] as [we] would like to be, filling in all the details of [our] desire and trying to accept the whole thing as a present reality, [we] would soon demonstrate that the control of affairs is from within out and not from without; the cause being that whatever exists as a mental picture in Mind must tend to, and finally does take form if the picture is really believed in and embodied... We should be careful to distinguish day dreaming and wistful wishing from really dynamic and creative treatment. When we treat we do not wish, we KNOW... THAT IT HAS ALREADY HAPPENED. We should think clearly and allow the image of our thoughts to sink into a subjective state. We do not crowd them down, we let them sink into this inner receptivity with power and with conviction. To hold thoughts, as though we were forcing issues,

150

does no good and utilizes a fraction of the creative power at our disposal. To hold in thought, as though we were LETTING something happen, is to use the greater power... the greatest power of all (Holmes, 1938, p 399)."

"Trained thought is far more powerful than untrained since the admission that thought is power gives it added power. This is one of the great secrets of Mental Science... We do not will, as though using an arbitrary force, we impress It. We should be careful to differentiate between these two attitudes of mind (Holmes, 1938, p 400)." Whatever becomes "established in the conscious mind... then [transmits] itself into a subjective embodiment and when this happens success will become habitual... Remember that when you use your subjective mind you are using the Creative Power of the Universe... There is but One Mind, whether It be individual or Universal (Holmes, 1938, p 400)."

"We must consciously know that we can use creative power. The more complete such acceptance on our part, the more completely we shall be able to use this power for definite purposes... If, at times, we doubt our ability to use the [Law], we should again remind our selves that it is not (Holmes, 1938, p 401)" the small "I" that does the work, but the greater "I"; the "I AM" that is in complete unity with the power of the Universe. "WE MUST BELIEVE. WE MUST LEARN HOW TO BELIEVE. WE SHOULD TREAT OURSELVES UNTIL WE BELIEVE. No one ever started at the top. Let us be happy to begin right where we are and grow (Holmes, 1938, p 401)."

"We attract to ourselves the objective form of our subjective embodiments (Holmes, 1938, p 401)." "Thoughts of lack, poverty and limitation contain within themselves the conditions necessary to produce lack, poverty and limitation... [The Law] will become to us what we are to It (Holmes, 1938, p 401)."

"Because all people have believed in lack a law of human thought has been made which binds the race.

Limitation is the result of an ignorant use of the Law... The real Law is one of freedom (Holmes, 1938, p 402)." When we learn to change what we have been bound to in the past, we "change the limitation into freedom. The two are merely a different use of the One Law (Holmes, 1938, p 402)."

"The Law of Mind is not selective. That is, It is receptive without caring what It receives. It is creative without caring what It creates... Thoughts of lack manifest as limitation. thoughts of abundance manifest as success and happiness. Failure and success are but two ends of one stick (Holmes, 1938, p 403)." I repeat here, for clarification purposes, that thought is only the beginning. What we truly manifest, success or failure, is based on the totality of what we embody.

"Fear is the reverse... attitude to faith, and is the result of a lack of faith... Fear arises from that... attitude which limits the possibility and the willingness of Spirit to give us the good we so greatly desire. There is nothing wrong in the desire for self-expression. God is more completely expressed through the [person] who lives largely than through one who lives meagerly (Holmes, 1938, p 404)." We need to grow our "field of faith... If it is God's pleasure to give us the Kingdom then it should be our privilege to accept the gift... The receiving of this gift is an eternal process of forever expanding the finite (Holmes, 1938, p 404)."

"The Infinite will not be, or become, less than Itself. We are of Its nature... Since Spirit is present in Its entirety at all times and in all places it follows, that all of Spirit is wherever we focus our attention. And since Spirit is both receptivity and creative responsiveness it follows that wherever we center our attention its image must concentrate substance into the form of such attention. This is fundamental to our concept of mental and spiritual treatment... Pure Spirit exists at the center of all form (Holmes, 1938, p 405)."

"If pure Spirit is at the center of everything and is always responding to [what we embody] there is no limit to Its manifestation for us except the limitations we set (Holmes,

1938, p 406)." Most of the limitations we set are unconscious, based on experiences long forgotten, race consciousness as close as our family or as far a field as generalities set by humanity over the centuries. Wherever our limitations come from, it is up to us to break the bonds of them and set ourselves free. "We cannot account for the seen without having faith in the unseen (Holmes, 1938, p 406)." No matter what the circumstances, we must take hold of the deeper Truth for us to break free from what holds us down. "The physical end is visible, the spiritual end invisible, but may be inwardly perceived and outwardly experienced (Holmes, 1938, p 407)." We are in unity with a "Universe [that] is a Spiritual System impregnated with Divine Ideas and peopled in Spiritual Forms (Holmes, 1938, p 407)."

"Each [of us] is in direct relationship to the Whole. Each [of us] is an image of God but God is not lessened by being represented in innumerable forms and through limitless numbers of mentalities any more than a figure five would become exhausted by being used by innumerable mathematicians. Our consciousness of God is our real self and at the same time it is both personal and impersonal. It is personal in that it is personified through us and it is impersonal in that we are all using a universal power. When we know that we are using such power all doubt as to our ability to use it will vanish and our words will be spoken with spontaneous reliance on Truth (Holmes, 1938, p 408)."

"Disease is neither person, place or thing to the one who wishes to heal. The practitioner must try to become conscious of perfection alone and nothing else (Holmes, 1938, p 408)." "The whole process is one of [embodiment] and realization and could not be anything else. The practitioner works within... until... satisfied... that [the] patient is now healed (Holmes, 1938, p 409)."

"[W]e are fulfilling our destiny when we think of ourselves as already Divine and perfect... This is what we mean by realization... It is an inward feeling, a silent sense of Divine

Reality (Holmes, 1938, p 409)." "After using whatever words will bring conviction to our [being] we pause and try to realize the presence of the All Power from which every special good comes... Wherever the image... is set, there the Power to create resides (Holmes, 1938, p 410)."

"When we bring a lamp into a darkened room, where does the darkness go? The darkness neither came nor did it go, anywhere. It never was a thing of itself, merely a condition. And we have power over our conditions... By merely bringing in the light the darkness vanished into its native nothingness. this is the power of Reality over seeming opposition or apparent separation (Holmes, 1938, p 410)."

"The relationship between the individual and the Universal Mind is one of reflection. That is, what we image for ourselves, It images for us... We can sit in the shade or move into the sunshine. Sitting in the shadow we may not really believe that there is sunshine. But the sun would be there all the time and all the time we are in bondage the real freedom exists (Holmes, 1938, p 411)."

"We attract to ourselves the objective likeness of (Holmes, 1938, p 411)" anything we fully embody. "The [embodiment] becomes the thing... If we believe in suffering we shall suffer... We should choose that which we wish to embody and by constant attention to it take on all its characteristics (Holmes, 1938, p 411)." This is another paradox in the teaching of the Science of Mind. The idea is to focus in a way that creates a calm assurance, a knowing that what we want will be created. When we focus willfully, we are using a forcefulness that actually means we embody an unknowing and think we alone have to create it instead of trusting Infinite Intelligence to create for us. So, we want to hold a mental equivalent of what we want, embody the essence of what we want, but then, with calm assurance that it is already done, release it to the One Mind and allow it to come into physical form.

"Life is a blackboard upon which we consciously or unconsciously write those messages which govern us... Spirit cannot be, or become, antagonistic toward us. It is always flowing into us and ever expressing Itself [as] us. This self-expression of [Spirit] is also the self-expression of [each of us] for the two are One. The "I AM" is both individual and universal. All individuality merges into universality. All forms are rooted in one common creative Mind and the Spirit of God is the Spirit of [humanity] (Holmes, 1938, p 412)."

"To practice the Presence of the Divine in others is to practice mental healing for it is the recognition of this Divine Presence that heals... In mental treatment we should feel as though the whole power of the universe were running through the words we speak. The words must become "Spirit and Life" if they are to overshadow the thoughts and actions that have brought about a discordant condition... The conviction that heals is that God is all in all and there is no other material cause and effect... Effective treatment must be independent of any existing circumstance whatsoever else it will never enter the realm of an Unconditioned Causation (Holmes, 1938, p 413)." There are those who say in our movement that we must turn away from the condition, but that is not what Dr. Holmes is saying here. We are not a movement of denial. Whatever our current experience, it is real and should not be denied. But, just because something is real in physical form, it can still be transformed the moment we see beyond the condition to the Truth. The Truth is that everything is made out of God. Any physical form is temporal. Each of us, out of what we embody, creates in each moment, the circumstances and conditions of our lives. So, by entering treatment and allowing the words and feelings to sink down into what we embody, we shift the physical form no matter what it was previously. This is how tumors disappear, miraculous situations appear and what others call impossible becomes inevitable. When we treat, it doesn't matter what the physical form is presently. What matters is that we recognize True Source, First Cause, God, as the only Power there is. As such, we are this Power, as there is nothing else but God. The moment we embody the words we speak, that which we speak must, of course, manifest.

"To have faith in God is to follow this faith through by having faith in the self. The real self is God and as such is to be implicitly trusted. The spark which burns at the center of our own soul is caught fem the living and eternal flame of the Spirit... There must come a time in our experience when we speak the conviction that is within us. This conviction of the Spiritual Universe in which we live is real and powerful... Each has been furnished with a divine torch whose wick burns from the oil of the eternal and ever renewing substance of faith in oneself and others. No good can come to us unless it makes its advent through the center of God Consciousness which we are (Holmes, 1938, p 414)."

"We must awake to the realization that a Divine Partnership has already been formed between the seen and the invisible (Holmes, 1938, p 415)." If this were not true, our thoughts would have no power and everything would rest on our physical shoulders to create. For those who believe this, life is a heavy burden. We, who know the True Power of the One Mind and ourselves as this Power, are free from the burden of carrying life's load alone. We can take comfort in knowing, as was stated consistently at the beginning of Dr. Holmes' radio show "there is a Power for good in the Universe, and we can use it."

"[T]he Law knows about us only that which we [embody] about ourselves. Therefore it makes all the difference in the world what we are impressing upon the Law as being true about ourselves. For if we [embody] poverty and lack we are certain creating them and causing them to be projected into our experience. If, on the other hand, we [embody] abundance, then the Law will as easily and willingly create abundance for us. It is all so simple that it seems unbelievable (Holmes, 1938, p 416)."

"To assert our individuality is to rise above the law of averages into the more highly specialized use of the Law which brings freedom rather than bondage, joy in the place of grief and wholeness instead of illness (Holmes, 1938, p 417)." This is one of the more wonderful benefits of practicing the Science of Mind. The more we immerse ourselves and embody our sense of Oneness, the greater our unique expression of the Divine. Our individualized creativity explodes through the use of Infinite Intelligence!

"If we believe that as isolated personalities we are able to heal... we shall be likely to fall into the error that it is human will that accomplishes the desired good (Holmes, 1938, p 417)." When we feel tired or unable to inspire ourselves, this is exactly what has occurred. "It is evident that we must not allow ourselves to think this way if we wish to accomplish anything worth while (Holmes, 1938, p 418)."

"The practitioner knows that the spiritual [person] needs no healing but that this has not yet become revealed... What the healer does is to... uncover and reveal the Truth of Being, which is that God is... every [person], and that this Indwelling Presence is already Perfect (Holmes, 1938, p 418)."

"A mystic is one who intuitively perceives Truth... What we have received from them constitutes the greatest intellectual and spiritual heritage of the ages (Holmes, 1938, p 418)." "All mystics have recognized the absolute unity of God and [humanity]. Within the Infinite Mind each individual exists, not as a separated, but as a separate and distinct entity. We are appoint in Universal Consciousness, which is God. We are not separated from Life, neither is It separated from us, but we are separate entities in It, individualized centers of God Consciousness (Holmes, 1938, p 419)."

"One of the most illuminating truths which mysticism has revealed is that there is no ultimate reality to evil. NO DEVIL, NO DAMNATION OUTSIDE OF ONE'S STATE OF THOUGHT, NO PUNISHMENT OUTSIDE OF THAT SELF-INFLICTED

THROUGH IGNORANCE, and no salvation outside of conscious co-operation with the Infinite. Consequently, they have taught that the answer to every problem is in man's own consciousness (Holmes, 1938, p 419)."

"Creation is the logical result of the outpush of Life into self-expression. It is the coming forth of Spirit into manifestation. The One encompasses and flows through All, spilling Itself into numberless forms, and personalities. These forms and personalities, propelled by the Cosmic Urge which brings them into being, have, within themselves, an impulse planted by the Divine; and since the Divine is Limitless and Perfect, It must and ultimately will bring all creation into a state of perfect manifestation (Holmes, 1938, p 420)."

"In flashes of illumination, the inspired have seen into the very center of Reality. They have been convinced of immortality now; of God as personal to the individual; of the inevitable overcoming of all evil by good (Holmes, 1938, p 421)." They have experienced the directive built into the fabric of everything that sings of Love, Harmony and Goodness. They have felt the gentle nudge and quieted themselves enough to answer the call. They have shared what they have experienced with humanity, so that all may drink from the same sacred cup, for those willing to listen.

"We comprehend the Infinite only to the degree that It expresses Itself [as] us, becoming... that which we believe it to be... The answer to every question is within [everyone], because [everyone] is within Spirit, and Spirit is an Indivisible Whole (Holmes, 1938, p 422)."

And so, we reach Dr. Ernest Holmes' final conclusion on the Science of Mind, written so beautifully and perfectly, I re-create it here in its entirety with no edits or comments.

"In conclusion, what the world needs is spiritual conviction, followed by spiritual experience. I would rather see a student of this Science prove its Principle than to have him repeat all the words of wisdom that have ever been uttered. It is far easier to teach the Truth than it is to practice It.

But the practice of Truth is personal to each, and in the long run no one can live our life for us. To each is given what [we need] and the gifts of heaven come alike to all. How we shall use these gifts is all that matters! To hold one's thought steadfastly to the constructive, to that which endures, and to the Truth, may no be easy in a rapidly changing world, but to the one who makes the attempt much is guaranteed.

The essence of spiritual mind healing- and of all true religious philosophy- is an inner realization of the Presence of Perfection within and around about. It is the hope of heaven, the Voice of God proclaiming: "I am that which thou art; thou art that which I am." (Holmes, 1938, p 423)."

Reference

Holmes, Ernest (1938). TheScience of Mind: A Philosophy, A Faith, A Way of Life. New York: Penguin Putnam Inc. Print

About the Author

Rev. Cliff Rubin is a Licensed Religious Science Minister and the Senior Minister at the YANA Virtual Center for Spiritual Living.

Introduced to these teachings by Dr.'s John and Barbara Waterhouse, Rev. Cliff was a member of the Asheville CSL for 17 years before starting his own center. During his tenure, he served in many capacities, including music director for 5 years.

He has been the guest speaker and musician at over 75 new thought churches and centers around the world. After 5 years of traveling, his very New York Jewish mother said to him, "So, why don't you become a minister?" He took his mother's wise advice.

YANA, an acronym for You Are Not Alone and in Sanskrit means "vehicle to enlightenment", is an online spiritual family To learn more about the YANA Virtual Center for Spiritual Living you can visit the website at http://yanavcsl.org. There, you will also find video recordings of Rev. Cliff's talks.

Rev. Cliff's 4 CD's of original new thought music have uplifted thousands. To hear his music you can visit http://cliffrubinmusic.com.